Ams

DIRECTIONS

WRITTEN AND RESEARCHED BY

Martin Dunford and Phil Lee

WITH ADDITIONAL RESEARCH BY

Karoline Densley

ROUGH GUIDES

NEW YORK • LONDON • DELHI

www.roughguides.com

Contents

Introduction to Amsterdam

This is as easy and engaging a capital city as you'll find – a compact, immediately likeable place, small enough to explore easily in a weekend, and with an intriguing combination of the parochial and the international. Just about everyone speaks good-to-fluent English, and more often than not more than a smattering of French and German as well.

Amsterdam is a thoughtful city too, with a long-standing liberal tradition that has given it a distinctive character, beginning with the obvious – the legalised prostitution and dope-

▸ Herengracht

▲ Leidseplein

smoking coffeeshops – through to the more subtle, encapsulated by Amsterdammers themselves in the Dutch word *gezellig*, which roughly corresponds to a combination of "cosy", "lived-in" and "warmly convivial". Nowhere is this more applicable than in the city's unparalleled selection of *gezellig* drinking establishments, whether you choose a traditional brown café or one of the newer, designer places. In addition, the city boasts dozens of great

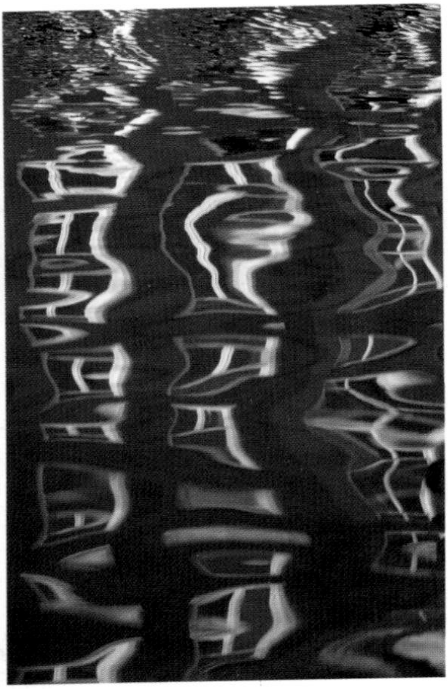
▲ Herengracht

restaurants, with its Indonesian cuisine second-to-none, and is at the forefront of contemporary European film, dance, drama and music. Amsterdam has several top-rank jazz venues – the Dutch have long had a soft spot for jazz – and the Concertgebouw concert hall is home to one of the world's leading orchestras. By comparison, the club scene is restrained by the standard of other big cities, although gay men are well catered for in the many gay bars and clubs, partly justifying Amsterdam's claim to be the "Gay Capital of Europe".

When to visit

Amsterdam enjoys a fairly standard temperate climate, with warm, if characteristically mild summers and moderately cold and wet winters. The climate is certainly not severe enough to make very much difference to the city's routines, which makes Amsterdam an ideal all-year destination. That said, high summer – roughly late June to August – sees the city's parks packed to the gunnels and parts of the centre almost overwhelmed by tourists, whereas spring and autumn are not too crowded and can be especially beautiful, with mist hanging over the canals and low sunlight beaming through the cloud cover. Indeed, Amsterdam has more than its fair share of cloudy days at any time of the year, but even in January and February, when things can be at their gloomiest, there are compensations – wet cobbles glistening under the street lights and the canals rippled by falling raindrops. In the summer, from around June to August, mosquitoes can be bothersome. At any time of the year, but particularly in summer, try to book your accommodation well ahead of time.

The layout of the city is determined by a web of canals radiating out from an historical core to loop right round the centre in a "Girdle of Canals", the Grachtengordel. This planned, seventeenth-century extension to the medieval town makes for a uniquely elegant urban environment, with tall gabled houses reflected in black-green waters. This is where the city is at its most beguiling, a world away from the traffic and noise of many another European city centre, and it has made Amsterdam one of the continent's most popular short-haul destinations. These charms are supplemented by a string of first-rate attractions, most notably the Anne Frankhuis, where the young Jewish diarist hid away during the German occupation of World War II, the Rijksmuseum, with its wonderful collection of Dutch paintings, including several of Rembrandt's finest works, and the peerless Vincent Van Gogh Museum, with the world's largest collection of the artist's work.

▸ Market stalls, Amsterdam

>> AMSTERDAM AT A GLANCE

Red Light District

Once upon a time this area was on the edge of the city. Now it's perhaps Amsterdam's most notorious neighbourhood, thronged with tourists and gangs of men here to ogle scantily clad prostitutes sitting in windows. It has to be seen, but it's worth bearing in mind that this is a business – rather than a tourist – district, with a solid bedrock of sleaze beneath the veneer of good, clean fun.

▸ Building detail, Grachtengordel

◂ Red Light District

Grachtengordel

The ultimate in thoughtful city planning, the Grachtengordel – basically the ring of canals that was dug around the medieval centre in the seventeenth century – tripled the city in size, and made Amsterdam what it is today. When anyone thinks of the city, it is these elegant waterways, criss-crossed by bridges, and flanked by tall quirkily gabled houses, that they have in mind.

De Pijp

The increasingly gentrified heart of working-class Amsterdam is worth visiting for its vibrant daily market and growing number of cool bars and eateries.

▲ Brouwersgracht warehouses, the Jordaan

Museum Quarter

Unsurprisingly, this area, just south of the city centre proper, is home to the cream of Amsterdam's museums. It is also one of the city's plusher neighbourhoods, with leafy streets and apartment blocks and upscale shops and restaurants. There are quite a few moderately priced hotels here too.

Western Canals and the Jordaan

In many ways this is the city centre's most appealing and restful area, with some of the most graceful stretches of the main canals, the more ramshackle small waterways of the Jordaan, and the tall warehouses of the former harbour area. All without pesky trams and traffic.

Old Jewish Quarter

Amsterdam's Jewish Quarter is not what it was – most of its inhabitants were deported during the Nazi occupation, and it's been unsympathetically redeveloped since then. But it holds a few fascinating corners of Jewish and wartime history as well as some key one-off attractions like the Rembrandthuis and the city's zoo.

Outside Amsterdam

Don't forget that Holland is a small country and that there are plenty of compelling attractions very close at hand – not least the small town of Haarlem, with the great Frans Hals Museum, and the stunning Keukenhof Gardens, among others.

▲ Joods Historisch Museum

Ideas

The big six sights

Amsterdam isn't a city of major sights; its pleasures lie in wandering the streets and taking in things aimlessly rather than targeting specific attractions. However there are a number of things you really shouldn't leave town without seeing, ranging from the high cultural hit of the Van Gogh Museum to the full-on sleaze of the Red Light District.

Anne Frank huis

The secret annexe in which the famous teenage diarist hid with her family during the Nazi occupation is perhaps the city's most popular – and most moving – tourist attraction.

▸ P.105 ▸ THE GRACHTENGORDEL ▲

Oude Kerk

The city centre's oldest church, now oddly surrounded by brothels.

▸ P.73 ▸ THE OLD CENTRE ▲

Royal Palace

The supreme architectural example of the Dutch empire at the height of its powers.

▸P.71 ▸ THE OLD CENTRE

Rijksmuseum

This is closed for a major restoration. But it's the city's greatest museum by far, featuring everything from paintings to furniture and applied arts. You can see the best of its paintings in a temporary home in the building's Philips Wing, as well as at the Nieuwe Kerk, Schiphol Airport and other places around town.

▸P.128 ▸ THE MUSEUM QUARTER AND THE VONDELPARK

Red Light District

Too steeped in the art of titillation to be truly shocking these days, but Amsterdam's red light district is still the real thing – and a big attraction in its own right.

▸P.72 ▸ THE OLD CENTRE

Van Gogh Museum

With the world's most comprehensive collection of the artist's work, this museum is simply unmissable.

▸P.130 ▸ THE MUSEUM QUARTER AND THE VONDELPARK

Brown cafés

Drinking your way around Amsterdam isn't such a bad way of passing the time, and the traditional Amsterdam bar – or brown café – is an excellent place to do just that. Named for the colour of their walls, stained by years of tobacco smoke, the city's brown cafés are cosy places to linger over a coffee, nurse a beer and read the paper. There's one on every corner, they're open all day, usually until late at night, and the atmosphere is relaxed and welcoming, whether you're a local or a tourist.

Hoppe

One of Amsterdam's longest established city-centre watering-holes.

▶ P.85 ▶ THE OLD CENTRE

De Reiger

Typical, buzzy, locals' bar in the Jordaan.

▶ P.113 ▶ THE WESTERN CANALS AND THE JORDAAN

Hegeraad

Perfectly preserved cosy brown café.

▸P.113 ▸ THE GRACHTENGORDEL ▲

Wynand Fockink

The city's best example of an old-fashioned *proeflokaal* or "tasting-house".

▸P.86 ▸ THE OLD CENTRE ▼

Restaurants

Amsterdam is definitely not a gourmet city. However there have always been great places to eat here, and the quality and number of establishments has risen over recent years. Whether it's hearty Dutch food, great fish or Indonesian specialities, you can eat superbly well nowadays if you know where to go.

Albatros

Something of an institution, and one of the city's best fish restaurants.

▶P.111 ▶ THE WESTERN CANALS AND THE JORDAAN ▲

Claes Claesz

A good place to sample proper Dutch food at moderate prices.

▸P.112 ▸ THE WESTERN CANALS AND THE JORDAAN ▼

De Silveren Spiegel

Arguably the best Dutch restaurant in the city, great for fish.

▸P83 ▸ THE OLD CENTRE ▼

Hoi Tin

Authentic Chinese restaurant in the heart of Amsterdam's rather dodgy Chinatown.

▸P.83 ▸ THE OLD CENTRE ▲

Keyser

Fin-de-siècle restaurant and café next door to the Concertgebouw.

▸P.134 ▸ THE MUSEUM QUARTER AND THE VONDELPARK ▲

Art galleries

The Dutch do art galleries better than most, and Amsterdam's house the prodigious output of the city's seventeenth-century Golden Age – Rembrandt, Frans Hals, Vermeer – as well as the work of Van Gogh and the modern movement. They're one of the highlights of the city, though sadly its greatest gallery – the Rijksmuseum – is closed for a long-term restoration.

Frans Hals Museum

It's not far to Haarlem to see the paintings of Frans Hals in the almshouses where he lived out his days.

▸P.145 ▸ DAY-TRIPS FROM AMSTERDAM

Van Gogh Museum

Not only the greatest collection of prints and paintings by Van Gogh, but also the nineteenth-century paintings and Japanese prints that influenced him.

▸P.130 ▸ THE MUSEUM QUARTER AND THE VONDELPARK

Rijksmuseum

Only partly open for the moment, this is the place to see the best of the city's collection of Rembrandts.

▸ P.128 ▸ THE MUSEUM QUARTER AND THE VONDELPARK ▲

CoBrA Museum

Cool modern museum hosting the art of the international CoBrA movement – made up of artists from Copenhagen, Brussels and Amsterdam.

▸ P.141 ▸ THE OUTER DISTRICTS ▼

Coffeeshops

Art, architecture and canals aside, many visitors to Amsterdam come for just one thing: drugs. Amsterdam remains one of the few cities in the world where you can smoke a joint in public. The places that you can do this – Amsterdam's euphemistically titled "coffeeshops" – are strictly controlled places that sell a wide variety of hash and grass in neat cellophane packets; they also sell spacecake (though aren't supposed to) as well as an array of soft drinks. The purchase and consumption of up to 5g of cannabis, and possession of up to 30g (the legal limit) are tolerated rather than legal – though it's unlikely that anything bad will happen to you if you step outside these limits.

Kadinsky

Chocolate chip cookies, good jazz and dope – what more could you want?

▸ P.110 ▸ THE WESTERN CANALS AND THE JORDAAN

Dampkring

Loud and friendly city-centre hangout.

P.81 ▸ THE OLD CENTRE

Rusland

Coffeshop is something of a misnomer for a place that's as well known for its tea as its dope.

P.81 ▸ THE OLD CENTRE

Greenhouse

Way out of the centre, but known for the quality of its offerings.

P.142 ▸ THE OUTER DISTRICTS

Siberië

Very relaxed and informal coffeeshop, slightly off the beaten tourist path.

P.110 ▸ THE WESTERN CANALS AND THE JORDAAN

Hostellers' Amsterdam

For those on a tight budget, Amsterdam's array of places offering dormitory accommodation is second to none – from official HI establishments to unofficial private hostels and even Christian hostels. Most will provide clean linen for a few euros extra or you should bring your own sleeping bag. Many also lock their guests out during the day, and there is sometimes a nightly curfew, though these are often late enough as to make no difference.

Hans Brinker

Very well-established and well-run hostel.

▸ P.162 ▸ THE GRACHTENGORDEL

Stay Okay Vondelpark

The best of the city's official hostels.

▸ P.162 ▸ THE MUSEUM QUARTER AND THE VONDELPARK

Flying Pig Palace

Well-maintained private hostel near the Vondelpark.

▸ P.162 ▸ THE MUSEUM QUARTER AND THE VONDELPARK ▲

Meeting Point

Cosy central hostel.

▸ P.161 ▸ THE OLD CENTRE ▲

Bulldog

Part of the coffeeshop chain, with everything from dorm beds to luxury apartments.

▸ P.161 ▸ THE OLD CENTRE ▼

International Budget

Small budget hotel situated on a quiet canal in the city centre.

▸ P.162 ▸ THE GRACHTENGORDEL ▼

Green Amsterdam

Perhaps because it is laced by canals, Amsterdam isn't an especially green city, but it does have one great city-centre green space in the Vondelpark, and any number of other verdant attractions on its limits or just outside.

Keukenhof Gardens

The largest flower garden in the world – bar none.

▸ P.147 ▸ DAY-TRIPS FROM AMSTERDAM ▲

Vondelpark

The leafy Vondelpark, with its ponds, footpaths and colony of parrots, is the city centre's most attractive park by a mile.

▸ P.132 ▸ THE MUSEUM QUARTER AND THE VONDELPARK ▲

Hortus Botanicus

A peaceful oasis in the heart of the city.

▸ P.121 ▸ THE OLD JEWISH QUARTER AND EASTERN DOCKS ▲

Zaanse Schans

This recreated Dutch village is one of the enticing sights on the edge of Amsterdam.

▸ P.149 ▸ DAY-TRIPS FROM AMSTERDAM ▼

Clubbers' Amsterdam

Clubbing in Amsterdam is not the exclusive, style-conscious business it is in many other capitals. There is no one really extravagant nightspot, and most Amsterdam clubs – even the hippest ones – aren't very expensive or difficult to get into. Music is mainly techno, and the most happening clubs tend to be on the outskirts of the city and come and go – see flyers and posters in bars for details. Most clubs charge around €10 to get in, often less during the week.

Escape

Home to Amsterdam's hottest weekend club nights.

▸ P.102 ▸ THE OUTER DISTRICTS

Mazzo

A varied agenda, at this, one of the city's hippest and most long-standing club venues.

▸ P.114 ▸ THE WESTERN CANALS AND THE JORDAAN

Melkweg

Still going strong since its heyday in the 1960s, hosting both club nights and live music.

▸ P.102 ▸ THE GRACHTENGORDEL ▲

Paradiso

Friday nights here are the city's best.

▸ P.102 ▸ THE GRACHTENGORDEL ▼

Kids' Amsterdam

With its canals, bikes and trams, Amsterdam can be entertaining enough for some kids. But there are several attractions aimed specifically at children, ranging from long-established places like the zoo – rated as one of the best in Europe – to circuses, ice-skating and city farms. Otherwise just rent a bike, or a canal bike, and take to the streets or water.

Artis Zoo

Unusually airy and open for an old city-centre zoo.

P.122 ▸ THE OLD JEWISH QUARTER AND EASTERN DOCKS

Circustheater Elleboog

Spend a day learning to juggle at this central venue.

▸P.101 ▸ THE GRACHTENGORDEL ▲

Kindermuseum (Tropenmuseum)

Ethnographic exhibits for kids – worthy but fun.

▸P.141 ▸ THE OUTER DISTRICTS ▼

Kinderkoekcafé

Yes, really, this is an entire restaurant run by children.

▸P.83 ▸ THE OLD CENTRE ▲

NEMO

Hands-on and interactive science museum.

▸P.125 ▸ THE OLD JEWISH QUARTER AND EASTERN DOCKS ▼

Gay Amsterdam

In keeping with the Dutch reputation for tolerance, no other city in Europe has historically accepted gay people quite as readily as Amsterdam. Here, perhaps more than anywhere else, it's possible to be openly gay and accepted by all of the straight community, and this attitude is reflected in a broad and long-standing gay infrastructure in the city: there are plenty of bars, clubs and services targeted at gay men and women.

Gay shopping

There's plenty on offer for gay shoppers in Amsterdam: book stores, video stores and a whole lot more.

▸P.81 ▸ THE OLD CENTRE ▲

IT

Probably the city's most glamorous gay night out.

▸ P.102 ▸ THE GRACHTENGORDEL ▼

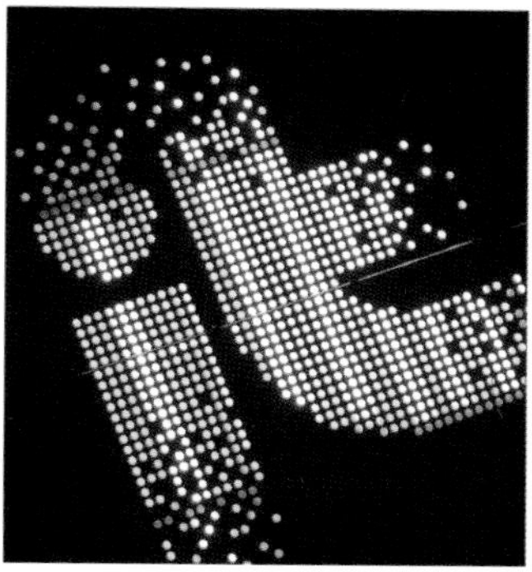

COC

Amsterdam branch of Holland's nationwide gay organization.

▸ P.114 ▸ THE WESTERN CANALS AND THE JORDAAN ▲

Homo-monument

This monument remembers gays and lesbians killed by the Nazis.

▸ P.106 ▸ THE WESTERN CANALS AND THE JORDAAN ▼

Festivals

Most of Amsterdam's festivals aren't so much street happenings as music and arts events. But there are one or two – Queen's Day is the big stand-out – which take over the city for a day or two, and others which have deep roots in the city's modern culture, most notably the Cannabis Cup and Gay Pride. It's not particularly worth timing your visit around any event, except perhaps Queen's Day, but if you're here at the right time it's worth knowing what's going on - contact the VVV for a full diary of year-round happenings.

Parade of St Nicolaas

The traditional parade of Santa Claus through the city, with his sidekicks, "Black Peters".

▸P.173 ▸ ESSENTIALS

Amsterdam Pride

A big celebration, given the size of the city's gay community.

▸P.172 ▸ ESSENTIALS

Cannabis Cup

Where else but Amsterdam would you find the world's annual dope awards?

▸P.173 ▸ ESSENTIALS

Queen's Day

The biggest event in the city's calendar, a wild affair in which everyone takes to the streets and waterways in an atmosphere of public celebration and organized debauchery.

▸P.171 ▸ ESSENTIALS

Canalside Amsterdam

Amsterdam's canals are its most distinctive feature, and you could spend many happy hours wandering from one to the other. Herengracht, Keizersgracht and Prinsengracht are the largest and best-known canals, girdling the city centre since they were added in the seventeenth century. Their gabled houses and numerous bridges are the Amsterdam you see in all the photos – and help to make this such a distinctive and beautiful city.

Golden Bend

The most opulent, though perhaps not the most characteristic, row of canal-houses in the city.

P.93 THE GRACHTENGORDEL

Leliegracht

One of the most charming of the radial stretches of water that connect the main canals.

P.105 THE WESTERN CANALS AND THE JORDAAN

Brouwersgracht

The former warehouses of this canal make it one of the city's most picturesque.

▸ P.103 ▸ THE WESTERN CANALS AND THE JORDAAN

Herengracht

The first of the canals to be dug for the city's planned seventeenth-century extension, and the one with the grandest buildings.

▸ P.93 ▸ THE GRACHTENGORDEL

Groenburgwal

Small dead-end canal right in the centre that is a lovely place to drink on a summer evening.

▸ P.76 ▸ THE OLD CENTRE

Markets

Amsterdam's not especially a shopping town but it has some great markets, from the famous fleamarket on Waterlooplein to smaller, more impromptu affairs selling books, organic produce, even pets. Devising a walk between the city's markets is a nice way of exploring the city centre.

Bloemenmarkt

This floating flower and plant market is a delight – and much cheaper than you might be used to back home.

▸ P.96 ▸ THE OLD CENTRE ▾

Albert Cuypmarkt

Busy general market that is still to some extent the authentic heart of working-class Amsterdam.

▸ P.139 ▸ THE OUTER DISTRICTS ▲

Waterlooplein

This fleamarket isn't what it was, but can still be a great source of clothing bargains.

▸ P.119 ▸ THE OLD JEWISH QUARTER AND EASTERN DOCK ▼

Boerenmarkt

The place to come for organic food goodies.

▸ P.108 ▸ THE WESTERN CANALS AND THE JORDAAN ▲

Oudemanhuispoort

A covered passageway lined with second-hand bookstalls.

▸ P.76 ▸ THE OLD CENTRE ▼

Special shopping

Variety is the essence of Amsterdam shopping. The city doesn't score particularly highly when it comes to big department stores and branches of the big-name designers. But it has a fantastic array of small stores specializing in everything from condoms to beads, all making for fantastic browsing between sights.

Kitsch Kitchen

Fancy kitchen accessories, all in the worst possible taste.

▸P.110 ▸ THE WESTERN CANALS AND THE JORDAAN

Donald E. Jongejans

Ancient spectacles, with and without lenses.

▸ P.110 ▸ THE WESTERN CANALS AND THE JORDAAN

Akkerman

The city's best pen specialist.

▸ P.79 ▸ THE OLD CENTRE

1001 Kralen

Nothing but beads in this Jordaan institution.

▸ P.110 ▸ THE WESTERN CANALS AND THE JORDAAN

Condomerie

The ultimate specialist shop, with a mind-boggling array of condoms.

▸ P.80 ▸ THE OLD CENTRE

Rembrandt

Born in Leiden in 1606, Rembrandt is widely regarded as the greatest artist of Holland's seventeenth-century Golden Age – no mean achievement in a century that wasn't exactly short of great artists. His mastery of historical subjects and his skilful rendering of portraits, meant he was the right painter at the right time for Amsterdam's self-promoting burghers. However, he fell from grace almost as quickly as he rose and it wasn't until the nineteenth century that his reputation recovered. His deft brushwork and imaginative approach to composition mean his reputation is as towering as ever.

Self-portrait

The artist in his pomp: young, well-dressed and going places.

▸P.131 ▸ THE MUSEUM QUARTER AND THE VONDELPARK

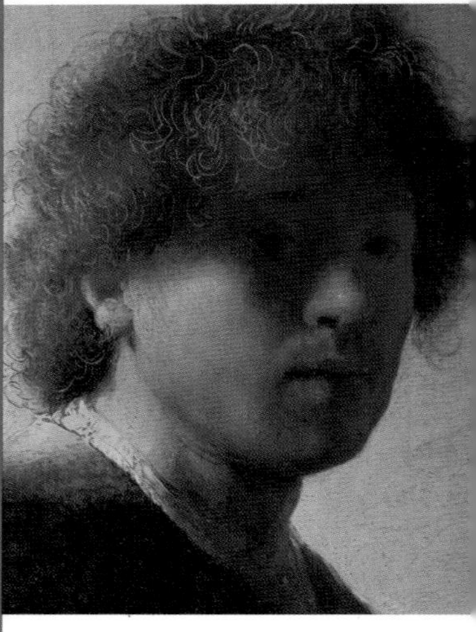

Self-portrait

The artist in his final years: beaten, bitter and close to the end.

▸P.131 ▸ THE MUSEUM QUARTER AND THE VONDELPARK

The Night Watch

Probably the most famous Rembrandt painting ever.

▶ P.130 ▶ THE MUSEUM QUARTER AND THE VONDELPARK ▲

The Jewish Bride

A study of marriage and duty – and love and tenderness.

▶ P.130 ▶ THE MUSEUM QUARTER AND THE VONDELPARK ▼

Designer bars

Not every Amsterdam bar is a brown café; indeed over recent years the trend has been to open bars and cafés that are anything but brown – bright, white places that are supposed to appeal to cool young people. They tend to come and go, but we've included a selection of the better established places.

Blincker

Hi-tech theatre bar on the edge of the Red Light District.

▸ P.85 ▸ THE OLD CENTRE

Lux

One of the city centre's trendiest bar hang-outs.

▸P.100 ▸ THE OLD CENTRE ▼

De Jaren

One of the largest and most inviting of the city's "grand cafés".

▸P.85 ▸ THE OLD CENTRE ▲

Het Land van Walem

Bright, modern city-centre stand-by.

▸P.100 ▸ THE GRACHTENGORDEL ▼

Morlang

Modern bar with occasional live music.

▸P.100 ▸ THE GRACHTENGORDEL ▲

Traditional architecture

Amsterdam's architecture is not of the huge, monumental variety. Long a republic, it doesn't boast palaces and other structures built to glorify its rulers. Rather, like the rest of Holland, its interest lies in the domestic, in the houses here that were built for the wealthy burghers of the Dutch Republic, and the details that lie therein. Some have been preserved and are open to visitors (see House Museums); others host homes and businesses and you have to be content to admire them from the outside.

Cromhouthuizen

Elegant seventeenth-century houses, built with all the soberness and frivolity of the age.

P.90 ▸ THE GRACHTENGORDEL

De Dolphijn

The home of the leader of the guard in Rembrandt's *The Night Watch*.

P.105 ▸ THE WESTERN CANALS AND THE JORDAAN

Felix Meritis Building

The city's best example of the Neo-classical style of the late eighteenth century.

▸ P.89 ▸ THE GRACHTENGORDEL ▲

Huis Bartolotti

One of the most handsome houses built on Herengracht during the Golden Age.

▸ P.107 ▸ THE WESTERN CANALS AND THE JORDAAN ▼

Herengracht 361–369

The best chance you'll get to compare gable styles.

▸ P.93 ▸ THE GRACHTENGORDEL ▼

Modern architecture

Amsterdam isn't all about old buildings; it has some interesting examples of twentieth-century architecture too, principally from the so-called Amsterdam School – whose style employed playful motifs and details in a modern context – as well as the odd example of the Art Deco and Art Nouveau styles.

American Hotel

The city's Art Nouveau masterpiece, now sadly renovated inside apart from its marvellous café.

▸ P.92 ▸ THE GRACHTENGORDEL

Beurs van Berlage

Clean, simple classic of the Dutch modern movement.

▸ P.70 ▸ THE OLD CENTRE ▼

Tuschinski

Extraordinarily well-preserved Art Deco cinema.

▸ P.95 ▸ THE GRACHTENGORDEL ▲

Scheepvaarthuis

Extravagantly building decorated with all things nautical – a good example of the decorative Amsterdam School.

▸ P.74 ▸ THE OLD CENTRE ▼

Het Schip

Classic apartment building of the Amsterdam School.

▸ P.110 ▸ THE WESTERN CANALS AND THE JORDAAN ▲

Churches

Amsterdam's skyline is punctured by the spires of its numerous churches. However, they're not one of the major attractions in this most Calvinist of cities. Some have been deconsecrated, and the interiors of the rest are plain and simple affairs more devoted to the practicalities of worship than extolling the glories of God. There are, however, one or two places that are worth seeking out.

Noorderkerk

The most spartan of Amsterdam's seventeenth-century churches.

▸ P.108 ▸ THE WESTERN CANALS AND THE JORDAAN

Amstelkring

Once a clandestine church for the city's Catholics, the seventeenth-century house chapel here is one of the city's most distinctive sights.

▸ P.73 ▸ THE OLD CENTRE ▲

Nieuwe Kerk

Despite its name, a fifteenth-century Gothic affair that is now just used for state occasions and exhibitions.

▸ P.71 ▸ THE OLD CENTRE ▲

Oude Kerk

Ancient Gothic church with fantastic sixteenth-century stained glass windows.

▸ P.73 ▸ THE OLD CENTRE ▼

Westerkerk

Amsterdam is celebrated for its soaring church spires, and this is one of its most striking.

▸ P.106 ▸ THE WESTERN CANALS AND THE JORDAAN ▼

What to eat

Dutch food tends to be higher in carbs than imagination, but there are one or two good, filling bar specialities that make a great option for lunch, and the odd streetfood delicacy that is definitely worth trying.

Herring

Tip your head back and swallow it, Dutch-style.

▸ P.142 ▸ THE OUTER DISTRICTS ▲

Frites with sauce

With mayonnaise, curry sauce or a host of other choices.

▸ P.82 ▸ THE OLD CENTRE ▲

Erwtensoep

Known as "snert", this thick pea soup is deliciously warming in winter.

P.112 ▸ THE WESTERN CANALS AND THE JORDAAN

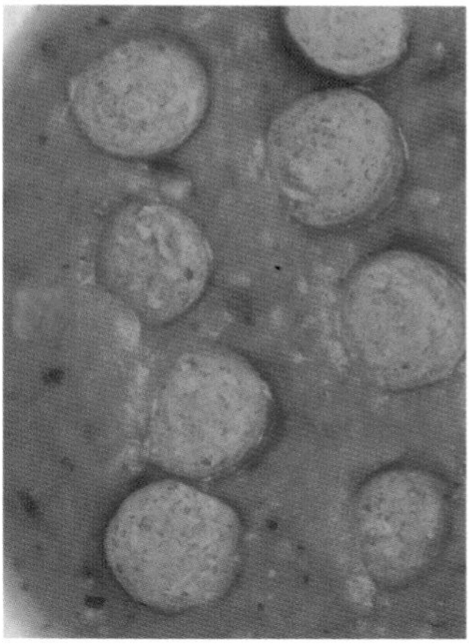

Indonesian food

Don't leave Amsterdam without trying one of its Indonesian restaurants – the most positive legacy of its colonial past.

P.98 ▸ THE GRACHTENGORDEL

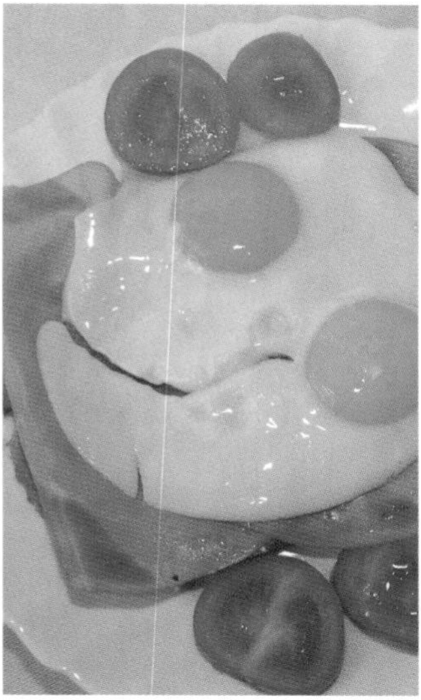

Uitsmijter

Fried eggs and ham or cheese.

P.113 ▸ THE WESTERN CANALS AND THE JORDAAN

Broodjes

Sandwiches and rolls basically, usually served open with pickles and salad.

P.82 ▸ THE OLD CENTRE

Clothes

When it comes to clothes, Amsterdam is in many ways an ideal place to shop: prices aren't too high and the city is sufficiently compact to save shoe leather. On the other hand, don't expect the choice of, say, London or New York. The city's department stores tend to be conservative, and the Dutch disapproval of ostentation means that the big international designers tend to stay away. What you will find are good-value if somewhat dull mainstream clothing along Kalverstraat, top-end stores on Van Baerlestraat and P.C. Hoofstraat – and plenty of quirky stuff in between.

Ksisk

Punky and funky fashions.

▸ P.96 ▸ THE GRACHTENGORDEL

Antonia

Dutch designer collections.

▸ P.96 ▸ THE GRACHTENGORDEL ▼

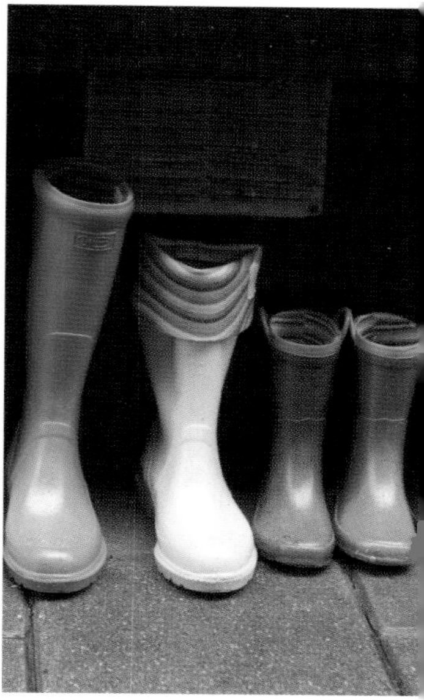

Edgar Vos

Holland's best-known high-end designer.

▸ P.133 ▸ THE MUSEUM QUARTER AND THE VONDELPARK ▲

Zipper

Vintage clothing selected with some style.

▸ P97 ▸ THE GRACHTENGORDEL ▼

Tearooms

Amsterdam's tearooms roughly correspond to the usual concept of a café – places that are generally open all day, might serve alcohol but definitely aren't bars, don't allow dope-smoking but provide good coffee, sandwiches, light snacks and cakes. Amsterdam is a walking city so you may be glad of one of these places if you're flagging.

Puccini

Great cakes and chocolates.

▸ P.84 ▸ THE OLD CENTRE ▲

Villa Zeezicht

The best apple cake in the city.

▸ P.82 ▸ THE OLD CENTRE ▲

Lunchcafé Winkel

Busy and friendly place to take the weight off on tours of the Jordaan.

▸P.111 ▸ THE WESTERN CANALS AND THE JORDAAN ▲

Metz

The department store's rooftop restaurant is the place to nurse a coffee and take in the views.

▸P.96 ▸ THE GRACHTENGORDEL ▼

Hotels

Accommodation in Amsterdam can be a major expense, but the city's compactness at least means that it is easy to stay somewhere central, even on a tight budget. Obviously the nicest thing to do is stay on one of the city's canals, preferably in a room facing the water, and there are some great places that you can do this. You'll pay a premium for the location, but at least when you wake up you'll know that you couldn't be anywhere else in the world.

Blakes

Part of the ultra-style-conscious Hempel chain hotel, with elegant rooms and suites fashioned out of a seventeenth-century canal house.

▸ P.157 ▸ THE GRACHTENGORDEL

Seven Bridges

A Rough Guide favourite, this moderately priced hotel has a great canalside location.

▸ P.158 ▸ THE GRACHTENGORDEL

Hotel de l'Europe

Grand old hotel that is perhaps the city centre's most luxurious option.

▸ P.156 ▸ THE OLD CENTRE

Prinsenhof

A top budget option in a great location.

▸ P.158 ▸ THE GRACHTENGORDEL

Toren

Lovely, moderately priced canal house hotel.

▸ P.159 ▸ THE GRACHTENGORDEL

Museums

Amsterdam excels with its museums – a huge variety, from restored aristocratic houses to museums devoted to history, science, shipping and ethnography. Bear in mind that most, especially those that are state-run, are shut on Mondays.

Nederlands Scheepvaart Museum

Homage to the Dutch mastery of the sea housed by the water in the old navy arsenal.

▸ P.124 ▸ THE OLD JEWISH QUARTER AND EASTERN DOCKS

Amsterdams Historisch Museum

The civic guard portraits of the Schuttersgalerij here provide an excellent introduction to this museum devoted to the life and times of the city.

▸ P.78 ▸ THE OLD CENTRE

Verzetsmuseum

This museum brilliantly charts the history of the Dutch resistance to the Nazis through a mixture of public and private exhibits.

▸ P.123 ▸ THE OLD JEWISH QUARTER AND EASTERN DOCKS

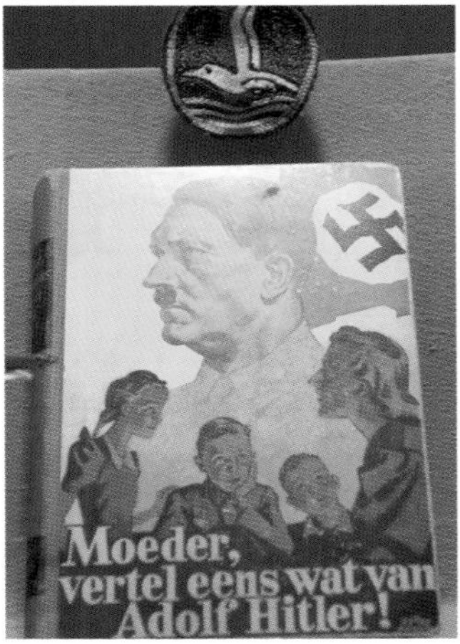

Museum Van Loon

Probably the best-preserved seventeenth-century canal house in the city.

▸ P.95 ▸ THE GRACHTENGORDEL

Museum Willet-Holthuysen

A glimpse of changing styles over the years since this canal house was built in 1685.

▸ P.93 ▸ THE GRACHTENGORDEL

Musical Amsterdam

There's no shortage of classical music concerts in Amsterdam, with two major orchestras based in the city, plus regular visits by touring outfits. Some of the city's churches host regular concerts, and there is top-notch opera, too, at the Muziektheater and Stadsschouwburg.

Concertgebouw

Home to the eponymous orchestra, and generally reckoned to have some of the best acoustics in the world.

▸ P.131 ▸ THE MUSEUM QUARTER AND THE VONDELPARK ▾

Stadsschouwburg

Theatre dance and opera predominate at this venue.

▸ P.91 ▸ THE GRACHTENGORDEL ▾

Carré Theatre

Grand old building on the Amstel that hosts everything from musicals to opera.

▸ P.175 ▸ THE GRACHTENGORDEL ▲

Waalse Kerk

A lovely venue for evening chamber concerts.

▸ P.86 ▸ THE OLD CENTRE ▼

Getting around

Almost all of Amsterdam's leading attractions are clustered in or near the city centre, within easy walking distance of each other. For longer jaunts, the city has a first-rate public transport system, comprising trams, buses, a pint-sized metro and numerous waterbourne alternatives. You might also want to do as the locals do and rent a bicycle: there are plenty of rental outlets, and with its well-integrated system of bicycle lanes, it couldn't be easier – or safer.

Museumboot/Canal buses

Canal boats link the major museums and other sights.

▶ P.166 ▶ ESSENTIALS

Bicycles

Get around like a local by renting a bike for the day.

▶ P.167 ▶ ESSENTIALS

Canal Bikes

These four-seater pedaloes can be rented by the hour, but it can take an age to get anywhere.

▶ P.167 ▶ ESSENTIALS ▲

Trams

The city's fifteen or so tram routes are the quickest way to get around the city.

▶ P.166 ▶ ESSENTIALS ▼

Places

Places

The Old Centre

Amsterdam's most vivacious district, the Old Centre is an oval-shaped affair whose tangle of antique streets and narrow canals is confined in the north by the River IJ and to the west and south by the Singel, the first of several canals that once girdled the entire city. Given the dominance of Centraal Station on most transport routes, this is where you'll almost certainly arrive. From here a stroll across the bridge will take you onto the Damrak, which divided the Oude Zijde (Old Side) of the medieval city to the east from the smaller Nieuwe Zijde (New Side) to the west. It also led – and leads – to the heart of the Old Centre, Dam Square, the site of the city's most imperial building, the Koninklijk Paleis (Royal Palace). The handsome seventeenth- and eighteenth-century canal houses that are more typical of the Old Centre are mostly concentrated in the Oude Zijde, which is also home to the world-famous Red-Light District.

Centraal Station

With its high gables and cheerful brickwork, Centraal Station is an imposing prelude to the city, built in the 1880s when it aroused much controversy because it effectively separated the centre from the River IJ, source of the city's wealth, for the first time in Amsterdam's long history. Outside, Stationsplein is a breezy open space, edged by ovals of water, packed with trams and dotted with barrel organs and chip stands, with street performers completing the picture in the summer.

St Nicolaaskerk

Prins Hendrikkade. Mon & Sat noon–3pm, Tues–Fri 11am–4pm. Free. The city's foremost Catholic church, with whopping twin towers and a cavernous interior. Above the altar is the crown of the Habsburg Emperor Maximilian, very much a symbol of the city and one you'll see again and again.

▼ CENTRAAL STATION

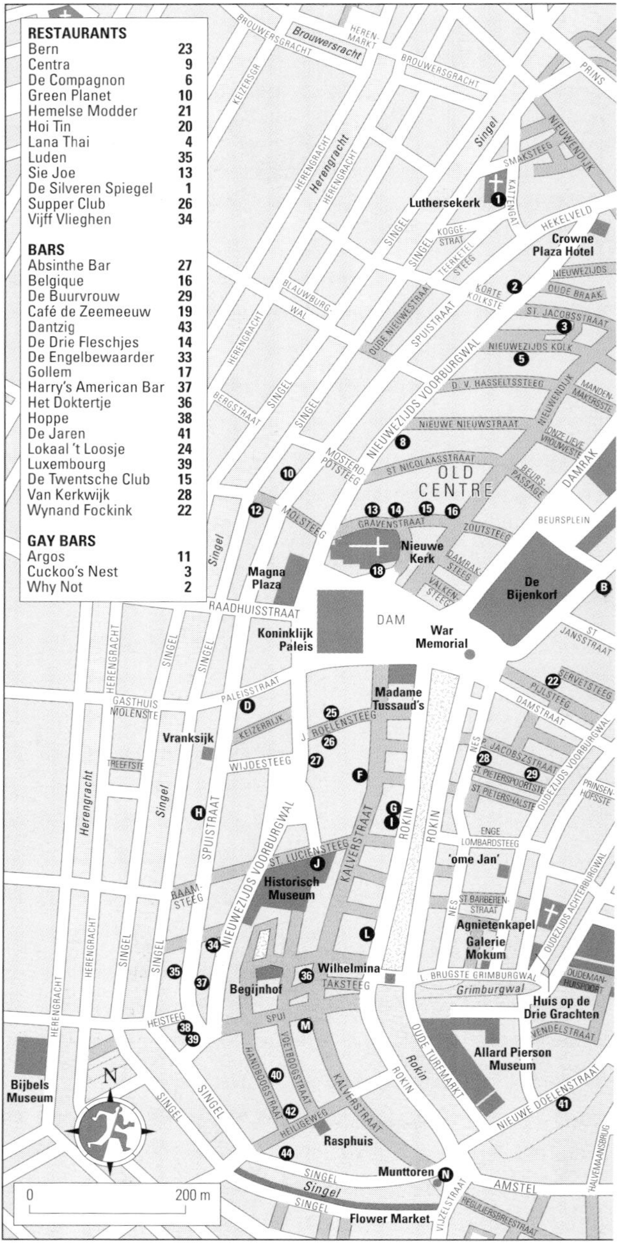
RESTAURANTS
Bern 23
Centra 9
De Compagnon 6
Green Planet 10
Hemelse Modder 21
Hoi Tin 20
Lana Thai 4
Luden 35
Sie Joe 13
De Silveren Spiegel 1
Supper Club 26
Vijff Vlieghen 34
BARS
Absinthe Bar 27
Belgique 16
De Buurvrouw 29
Café de Zeemeeuw 19
Dantzig 43
De Drie Fleschjes 14
De Engelbewaarder 33
Gollem 17
Harry's American Bar 37
Het Doktertje 36
Hoppe 38
De Jaren 41
Lokaal 't Loosje 24
Luxembourg 39
De Twentsche Club 15
Van Kerkwijk 28
Wynand Fockink 22
GAY BARS
Argos 11
Cuckoo's Nest 3
Why Not 2
Brouwersgracht
BROUWERSGRACHT
HEREN-MARKT
PRINS
KEIZERSGR
HERENGRACHT
Herengracht
Singel
SINGEL
NIEUWENDIJK
SMAKSTEEG
KATTENGAT
Luthersekerk
HEKELVELD
Crowne Plaza Hotel
KOGGE-STRAAT
TEERKETEL-STEEG
NIEUWEZIJDS
OUDE BRAAK
KORTE KOLKSTEEG
BLAUWBURG-WAL
OUDE NIEUWSTRAAT
SPUISTRAAT
ST. JACOBSSTRAAT
NIEUWEZIJDS KOLK
NIEUWEZIJDS VOORBURGWAL
D. V. HASSELTSSTEEG
MANDEN-MAKERSSTEEG
BERGSTRAAT
NIEUWE NIEUWSTRAAT
ONZE LIEVE VROUWESTEEG
MOSTERD-POTSTEEG
ST NICOLAASSTRAAT
OLD CENTRE
BEURS-PASSAGE
DAMRAK
MOLSTEEG
GRAVENSTRAAT
ZOUTSTEEG
BEURSPLEIN
Nieuwe Kerk
DAMRAK-STEEG
VALKEN-STEEG
Magna Plaza
De Bijenkorf
RAADHUISSTRAAT
DAM
Koninklijk Paleis
War Memorial
ST JANSSTRAAT
SERVETSTEEG
PIJLSTEEG
Madame Tussaud's
PALEISSTRAAT
GASTHUIS MOLENSTEEG
DAMSTRAAT
KEIZERRIJK
J. ROELENSTEEG
Vranksijk
NES
ST JACOBSZSTRAAT
WIJDESTEEG
TREEFTSTEEG
ST PIETERSPOORTSTEEG
ST PIETERSHALSTEEG
OUDEZIJDS VOORBURGWAL
PRINSEN-HOFSSTEEG
KALVERSTRAAT
ROKIN
ENGE LOMBARDSTEEG
ST. LUCIENSTEEG
'ome Jan'
Historisch Museum
RAAMSTEEG
ST BARBERENSTRAAT
OUDEZIJDS ACHTERBURGWAL
Agnietenkapel
Galerie Mokum
Wilhelmina
TAKSTEEG
L. BRUGSTE GRIMBURGWAL
Grimburgwal
Begijnhof
OUDEMAN-HUISPOORT
Huis op de Drie Grachten
HEISTEEG
SPUI
VENDELSTRAAT
HANDBOOGSTRAAT
VOETBOOGSTRAAT
OUDE TURFMARKT
Rokin
Allard Pierson Museum
N
Bijbels Museum
HEILIGEWEG
NIEUWE DOELENSTRAAT
Rasphuis
HALVEMAANSBRUG
Munttoren
AMSTEL
VIJZELSTRAAT
REGULIERSBREESTRAAT
Flower Market
0
200 m

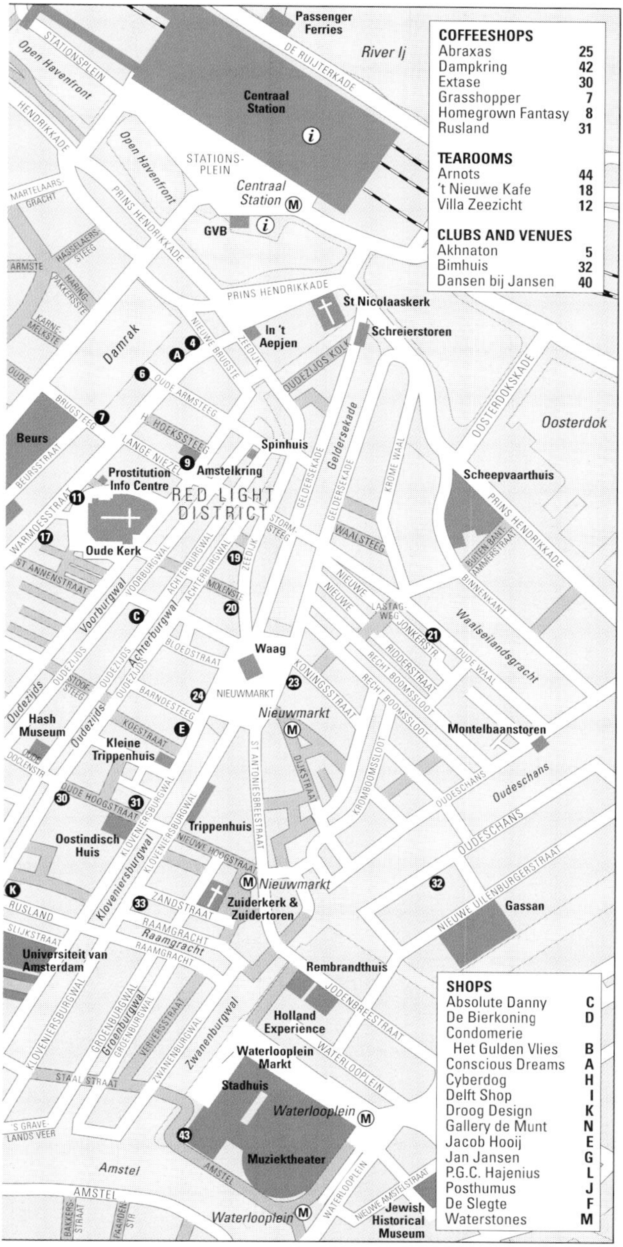
COFFEESHOPS
Abraxas 25
Dampkring 42
Extase 30
Grasshopper 7
Homegrown Fantasy 8
Rusland 31
TEAROOMS
Arnots 44
't Nieuwe Kafe 18
Villa Zeezicht 12
CLUBS AND VENUES
Akhnaton 5
Bimhuis 32
Dansen bij Jansen 40
SHOPS
Absolute Danny C
De Bierkoning D
Condomerie Het Gulden Vlies B
Conscious Dreams A
Cyberdog H
Delft Shop I
Droog Design K
Gallery de Munt N
Jacob Hooij E
Jan Jansen G
P.G.C. Hajenius L
Posthumus J
De Slegte F
Waterstones M
Passenger Ferries
River Ij
Centraal Station
STATIONSPLEIN
Centraal Station
GVB
Open Havenfront
PRINS HENDRIKKADE
St Nicolaaskerk
Schreierstoren
In 't Aepjen
Damrak
Beurs
Spinhuis
Amstelkring
Prostitution Info Centre
RED LIGHT DISTRICT
Oude Kerk
Geldersekade
Oosterdok
Scheepvaarthuis
Waalseilandsgracht
Waag
NIEUWMARKT
Nieuwmarkt
Hash Museum
Kleine Trippenhuis
Montelbaanstoren
Oudeschans
Trippenhuis
Oostindisch Huis
Kloveniersburgwal
Zuiderkerk & Zuidertoren
Nieuwmarkt
Gassan
Universiteit van Amsterdam
Raamgracht
Rembrandthuis
Holland Experience
Waterlooplein Markt
Stadhuis
Waterlooplein
Muziektheater
Amstel
Waterlooplein
Jewish Historical Museum

Damrak

Running from Centraal Station to Dam square, Damrak was a canal until 1672, when it was filled in – much to the relief of the locals, who were tired of the stink. Formerly, the canal had been the city's main nautical artery, with boats sailing up it to discharge their goods right in the centre of town on Dam square. Thereafter, with the docks moved elsewhere, Damrak became a busy commercial drag, as it remains today, a wide but unenticing avenue lined with tacky restaurants, bars and bureaux de change.

The Beurs van Berlage

Damrak ⓦwww.beursvanberlage.nl. Usually Tues–Sun 11am–5pm. The imposing bulk of the Beurs – the old Stock Exchange – is a seminal work designed at the turn of the twentieth century by the leading light of the Dutch modern movement, Hendrik Petrus Berlage. Berlage re-routed Dutch architecture with this building, forsaking the historicism that had dominated the nineteenth century and opting for a style with cleaner, heavier lines. The Beurs has long since lost its commercial function and today it's used for exhibitions, concerts and conferences, which means that sometimes you can go in, sometimes you can't. Inside, the main hall is distinguished by the graceful lines of its exposed ironwork and its shallow-arched arcades as well as the fanciful frieze celebrating the stockbroker's trade.

Dam square

It was Dam square that gave Amsterdam its name: in the thirteenth century the River Amstel was dammed here, and the fishing village that grew around it became known as "Amstelredam". Boats could sail into the square down the Damrak and unload right in the middle of the settlement, which soon prospered by trading herrings for Baltic grain. Today it's an open and airy but somehow rather desultory square, despite – or perhaps partly because of – the presence of the main municipal war memorial, a prominent stone tusk adorned by bleak, suffering figures and decorated with the coats of arms of each of the Netherlands'

▼ DAMRAK

provinces (plus the ex-colony of Indonesia). The Amsterdam branch of **Madame Tussaud's** waxworks is on the Dam, at no. 20 (daily: July–Aug 9.30am–8.30pm; Sept to June 10am–6.30pm; last entry 1hr before closing; €22.50, children 5–15 €10, over 60s €17.50; Ⓦwww.madametussauds.nl).

The Koninklijk Paleis

Dam Ⓣ020/620 4060, Ⓦwww.koninklijkhuis.nl. Hours vary, but normally include Tues–Thurs 12.30–5pm. €4.50. Dominating Dam square is the Koninklijk Paleis (Royal Palace), though the title is deceptive, given that this vast sandstone structure started out as the city's Stadhuis (town hall), and only had its first royal occupant when Louis Bonaparte, brother of Napoleon, moved in during the French occupation. At the time of the building's construction in the mid-seventeenth century, Amsterdam was at the height of its powers and the city council craved a residence that was a suitable declaration of its wealth and independence. They opted for a progressive design by Jacob van Campen, and in 1648 work started on what was then the largest town hall in Europe, supported by no less than 13,659 wooden piles driven into the Dam's sandy soil.

The exterior is very much to the allegorical point with depictions of Amsterdam as a port and trading centre, that at the front presided over by Neptune and a veritable herd of unicorns. Above these panels are representations of the values the city council espoused – at the front, Prudence, Justice and Peace, to the rear Temperance, and Vigilance to either side of a muscular, globe-carrying Atlas. One deliberate precaution, however, was the omission of a central doorway – just in case the mob turned nasty and stormed the place.

Inside, the **Citizen's Hall** is the most remarkable room, a handsome arcaded marble chamber where the enthroned figure of Amsterdam looks down on three circular maps, one each of the eastern and western hemispheres, the other of the northern sky. Other allegorical figures ram home the municipal point: flanking "Amsterdam" are strength and wisdom and on the left the god Amphion plays his lyre to persuade the stones to pile themselves up into a wall as an example of good government. There are witty touches too – cocks fight above the entrance to the Commissioner of Petty Affairs, while Apollo, god of the sun and the arts, brings harmony to the disputes; and a relief in the Bankruptcy Chamber shows the Fall of Icarus, surrounded by marble carvings depicting hungry rats scurrying around an empty chest and unpaid bills.

The Nieuwe Kerk

Dam Ⓣ020/638 6909, Ⓦwww.nieuwekerk.nl. Daily 10am–6pm. Vying for importance with the Royal Palace is the adjacent Nieuwe Kerk, which despite its name – literally "new church" – is an early fifteenth-century structure built in a late flourish of the Gothic style, with a forest of pinnacles and high, slender gables. The interior is a hangar-like affair, now de-sanctified and used for temporary exhibitions. Amongst a scattering of decorative highlights, look out for the seventeenth-century tomb of

Dutch naval hero Admiral Michiel de Ruyter, complete with trumpeting angels, conch-blowing Neptunes and cherubs all in a tizzy. Ruyter was buried here with full military honours and the church is still used for state occasions: the coronations of queens Wilhelmina, Juliana and, in 1980, Beatrix, were all held here.

Magna Plaza

Nieuwezijds Voorburgwal, ⓦwww.magnaplaza.nl. Daily 10am–7pm. Behind the Royal Palace, you can't miss the old neo-Gothic post office of 1899, now converted into the Magna Plaza shopping mall. The building is a grand affair, and makes an attractive setting for numerous clothes chains that now inhabit its red-brick interior.

The Red Light District

The area immediately to the east of Damrak is the Red Light District, known locally as "De Walletjes" (Small Walls) on account of the series of low brick walls that contains its canals. The district stretches across the two narrow canals that once marked the eastern part of medieval Amsterdam, Oudezijds Voorburgwal and Oudezijds Achterburgwal. Effectively the main drags of the Red Light area, both of these streets are distinctly seedy, though the legalized prostitution here has long been one of the city's most distinctive draws.

The two canals, with their narrow connecting passages, are thronged with "window brothels" and at busy times the crass, on-street haggling over the price of sex is drowned out by a surprisingly festive atmosphere – entire families grinning more or less amiably at the women in the windows or discussing the specifications (and feasibility) of the sex toys in the shops. There's a nasty undertow to the district though, oddly enough sharper during the daytime, when the pimps hang out in shifty gangs and drug addicts wait anxiously, assessing the chances of scoring their next hit. Don't even think about taking a picture of a "window brothel" unless you're prepared for some major grief from the camera-shy prostitutes.

Oude Kerk

Oudekerksplain. Mon–Sat 11am–5pm, Sun 1–5pm. €4. The Gothic Oude Kerk is the city's most appealing church. There's been a church on this site since the middle of the thirteenth century, but most of the present building dates from a century later, funded by the pilgrims

▼ RED LIGHT DISTRICT

who came here in their hundreds following a widely publicized miracle. The story goes that, in 1345, a dying man regurgitated the Host he had received here at Communion and when it was thrown on the fire afterwards, it did not burn. The unburnable Host was placed in a chest and eventually installed here, and although it disappeared during the Reformation, thousands of the faithful still come to take part in the annual commemorative Stille Omgang in mid-March, a silent nocturnal procession terminating at the Oude Kerk. Inside you can see the unadorned memorial tablet of Rembrandt's first wife, Saskia van Uylenburg, and three beautifully coloured stained-glass windows beside the ambulatory dating from the 1550s. They depict, from left to right, the Annunciation, the Adoration of the Shepherds and the Dormition of the Virgin.

The Amstelkring

Oudezijds Voorburgwal 40. Mon–Sat 10am–5pm, Sun 1–5pm. €7. The front of the Oude Kerk overlooks the northern reaches of Oudezijds Voorburgwal, whose handsome facades recall ritzier days when this was one of the wealthiest parts of the city, richly earning its nickname the "Velvet Canal". A few metres north of the Oude Kerk is the clandestine Amstelkring, a former Catholic church, now one of Amsterdam's most enjoyable museums. The Amstelkring – "Amstel Circle" – is named after the group of nineteenth-century historians who saved the building from demolition, but its proper name is Ons Lieve Heer Op Solder ("Our Dear Lord in the Attic"). The church dates from the early seventeenth

▼ AMSTELKRING INTERIOR

century when, with the Protestants firmly in control, the city's Catholics were only allowed to practise their faith in secret – as here in this clandestine church, which occupies the loft of a wealthy merchant's house. The church's narrow nave has been skilfully shoehorned into the available space and, flanked by elegant balconies, there's just enough room for an ornately carved organ at one end and a mock-marble high altar, decorated with Jacob de Wit's mawkish *Baptism of Christ*, at the other. The rest of the house is similarly untouched, its original furnishings reminiscent of interiors by Vermeer or De Hooch.

Nieuwmarkt

The Nieuwmarkt, a wide open cobbled square that was long one of the city's most important markets, has as its main focus the multi-turreted Waag, a delightful building dating from the 1480s, when it served as one of the city's fortified gates, Sint Antoniespoort, before being turned into a municipal weighing-house (*waag*), with the rooms upstairs taken over by the surgeons' guild. It was here that the surgeons held lectures on anatomy and public dissections, the inspiration for Rembrandt's famous *Anatomy Lesson of Dr Tulp*. The *waag* has now been converted into a café-bar and restaurant, *In de Waag*.

▼ THE WAAG

Leaving the Nieuwmarkt, there's a choice of three tempting routes: southeast along St Antoniesbreestraat to the Old Jewish Quarter (see p.115); south along Kloveniersburgwal to the Trippenhuis and the Hash Museum (see opposite and p.76); and north along Geldersekade to the Schreierstoren and the Stedelijk Museum.

The Schreierstoren

Geldersekade. Squat Schreierstoren (Weepers' Tower) is a rare surviving chunk of the city's medieval wall. Originally, the tower overlooked the River IJ and it was here that women gathered to watch their menfolk sail away – hence its name. An old and badly weathered stone plaque inserted in the wall is a reminder of all those sad goodbyes, and another much more recent plaque recalls the departure of Henry Hudson from here in 1609, when he stumbled across an island the locals called Manhattan.

Het Scheepvaarthuis

Prins Hendrikkade 108. Completed in 1917, this almost neurotic edifice is covered with a welter of decoration celebrating the city's marine connections – the entrance is shaped like the prow of a ship, and surmounted by statues of Poseidon and his wife and representations of the four points of the compass.

Stedelijk Museum

Oosterdokskade 3 ⓣ020/573 2737, ⓦwww.stedelijk.nl. No opening times available at time of going to print. €8.
The Stedelijk Museum has long been Amsterdam's number-one venue for modern art. Its

permanent collection is wide-ranging and its temporary exhibitions are usually of international standard. It's been housed in a large old building on Paulus Potterstraat out near the Rijksmuseum (see p.128) for years, but its old home is presently being gutted and won't be open again until 2008. In the meantime, the former postal building on Oosterdokskade near Centraal Station has been pressed into service to accommodate the main body of the permanent collection. It seems a good choice – the building is a fetching office block dating from the 1960s – for a permanent collection that includes drawings by Picasso, Matisse and their contemporaries, and paintings by Manet, Monet, Bonnard, Ensor, Cézanne, and of course Mondriaan, from his early, muddy-coloured abstractions to the cool, boldly coloured rectangular blocks for which he's most famous. The museum also has a good sample of the work of Kasimir Malevich, his dense attempts at Cubism leading to the dynamism and bold, primary tones of his "Suprematist" paintings, several Marc Chagall paintings, and a number of pictures by American Abstract Expressionists Mark Rothko, Ellsworth Kelly and Barnett Newman, plus works by other American artists – Lichtenstein, Warhol, Jean Dubuffet.

Kloveniersburgwal

Nieuwmarkt lies at the northern end of Kloveniersburgwal, a long, dead-straight waterway framed by a string of old and dignified facades that was the outermost of the three eastern canals of the medieval city. One house of special note here is the **Trippenhuis**, at no. 29, a huge overblown mansion complete with Corinthian pilasters and a grand frieze built for the Trip family in 1662. One of the richest families in Amsterdam, the Trips were long a powerful force among the Magnificat, the clique of families (Six, Trip, Hooft and Pauw) who shared power during the city's Golden Age. Almost directly opposite, on the west bank of the canal, the **Kleine Trippenhuis**, at no. 26, is, by contrast, one of the narrowest houses in Amsterdam, albeit with a warmly carved facade with a balustrade featuring centaurs and sphinxes. Legend asserts that Mr Trip's coachman was so taken aback by the size of the new family mansion that he exclaimed he

▲ KLEINE TRIPPENHUIS

would be happy with a home no wider than the Trips' front door – which is exactly what he got; his reaction to his new lodgings is not recorded.

Hash Marihuana Hemp Museum

Oudezijds Achterburgwal 148 ⓦwww.hashmuseum.com. Daily 11am–10pm. €5.70. The Hash Marihuana Hemp Museum is still going strong, despite intermittent battles with the police. It features displays on different kinds of dope and the huge number of ways to imbibe and otherwise use it. It has an indoor marijuana garden, samples of textiles and paper made with hemp, and pamphlets explaining the medicinal properties of cannabis. There's also a shop selling pipes, books, videos and plenty of souvenirs.

Oudemanhuispoort and around

Doubling back to Kloveniersburgwal, turn right for the Oudemanhuispoort, a covered passageway leading off the street that is lined with secondhand bookstalls (Mon–Sat 10am–4pm), was formerly part of an almshouse complex for elderly men – hence the unusual name. Just beyond, at the south end of Kloveniersburgwal, lies one of the prettiest corners of the city, a small pocket of placid waterway and old canal houses that extends east to Groenburgwal and west to Grimburgwal.

Rokin and Kalverstraat

Rokin picks up where the Damrak leaves off, cutting south from Dam Square in a wide sweep that follows the former course of the River Amstel. This was the business centre of the nineteenth-century city, and although it has lost much of its prestige it is still flanked by an attractive medley of architectural styles incorporating everything from grandiose nineteenth-

▼ HASH MUSEUM

century mansions to more utilitarian modern stuff. Running parallel, pedestrianized **Kalverstraat** is a hectic shopping street that has been a commercial centre since medieval times, when it was used as a calf market; nowadays it's home to many of the city's chain stores and clothes shops.

▼ ALLARD PIERSON MUSEUM

Allard Pierson Museum

Oude Turfmarkt 127. Tues–Fri 10am–5pm, Sat & Sun 1–5pm. €4.30.
A good old-fashioned archeological museum in a solid Neoclassical building dating from the 1860s, the Allard Pierson Museum holds a wide-ranging albeit fairly small collection of finds retrieved from the Middle East, plus Egypt, Greece and Italy. The particular highlights are the museum's Greek pottery, with fine examples of both the black- and red-figured wares produced in the sixth and fifth centuries BC, and several ornate Roman sarcophagi.

Heiligeweg and Spui

Workaday **Heiligeweg**, or "Holy Way", was once part of a much longer route used by pilgrims heading into Amsterdam. Every other religious reference disappeared centuries ago, but there is one interesting edifice here, the fanciful gateway of the old Rasphuis (House of Correction) that now fronts a shopping mall at the foot of Voetboogstraat. The gateway is surmounted by a sculpture of a woman punishing two criminals chained at her sides above the single word "Castigatio" (punishment). Beneath is a carving by Hendrik de Keyser showing wolves and lions cringing before the whip.

Cut up Voetboogstraat and you soon reach the **Spui**, whose west end opens out into a wide, tram-clanking square flanked by bookshops and cafés. In the middle is a cloying statue of a young boy, known as 't Lieverdje ("Little Darling" or "Loveable Scamp"), a gift to the city from a cigarette company in 1960. It was here in the mid-1960s, with the statue seen as a symbol of the addicted consumer, that the playful political mavericks, the

▼ MUNTTOREN

▲ THE BEGIJNHOF

Provos, organized some of their most successful public *ludiek* (pranks). There's a small secondhand book market here on Friday mornings.

The Begijnhof

Daily 10am–5pm; free. A little gateway on the north side of the Spui leads into the Begijnhof, where a huddle of immaculately maintained old houses looks onto a central green; if this door is locked, try the main entrance, just a couple of hundred metres north of the Spui on Gedempte Begijnensloot. The Begijnhof was founded in the fourteenth century as a home for the *beguines* – members of a Catholic sisterhood living as nuns, but without vows and with the right of return to the secular world. The original medieval complex comprised a series of humble brick cottages, but these were mostly replaced by the larger, grander houses of today shortly after the Reformation, though the secretive, enclosed design survived.

The Engelse Kerk which takes up one side of the Begijnhof is of medieval construction, but it was taken from the *beguines* and given to Amsterdam's English community during the Reformation and is of interest for its carefully worked pulpit panels, several of which were designed by a youthful Piet Mondriaan. The *beguines*, meanwhile, celebrated Mass inconspicuously in the clandestine Catholic chapel (Mon 1–6pm, Tues–Sun 9am–6pm; free), which they established in the house opposite their old church, and this is still used today, a homely little place with some sentimental religious paintings.

Amsterdams Historisch Museum

Two entrances: Nieuwezijds Voorburgwal 357 or Kalverstraat 92, ⓦ www.ahm.nl. Mon–Fri 10am–5pm, Sat & Sun 11am–5pm. €6. A few metres from the Begijnhof, the open-access and free Schuttersgalerij – the Civic Guard Gallery – is lined by an interesting assortment of group portraits of the Amsterdam militia, painted when the city was at the height of its economic success. The gallery is actually part of the adjoining Amsterdams Historisch Museum, which occupies the smartly restored but rambling seventeenth-century buildings of the municipal orphanage. This museum surveys the city's development with a scattering of artefacts and lots of paintings from the thirteenth century onwards – a somewhat garbled collection, but at least the labelling is in English and Dutch. High points include a number of paintings from the city's Golden Age – Rembrandt's wonderful *Anatomy Lesson of Dr Jan Deijman* stands out – and the section entitled "Social Care & Stern Discipline". Here, the harsh paternalism of the city's merchant oligarchy is examined and there are paintings depicting the regents of several orphanages, self-contented bourgeois in the company of the grateful poor.

Shops

Absolute Danny

O.Z. Achterburgwal 78 ☎020/421 0915. You can't visit the Red-Light District without visiting at least one sex shop. This one bills itself as an "erotic lifestyle store", with everything that implies.

Akkerman

Kalverstraat 149 ☎020/623 1649. The city's poshest pen shop.

De Bierkoning

Paleisstraat 125 ☎020/625 2336. The "Beer King" is aptly named: 950 different beers, with the appropriate glasses to drink them from – just in case you thought beer-drinking could be taken lightly.

De Bijenkorf

Dam 1 ☎020/552 1700. Dominating the northern corner of Dam square, this is the city's top department store, a huge bustling place whose name means bee-hive. Curiously, De Bijenkorf posed all sorts of problems for the Germans when they first occupied the city in World War II. It was a Jewish concern, so the Nazis didn't really want their troops shopping here, but it was just too popular to implement a total ban; the bizarre solution was to prohibit German soldiers from shopping on the ground floor, where the store's Jewish employees were concentrated, as they always had been, in the luxury goods section. Nowadays the sections to head for include household goods, cosmetics and kidswear; there's also a good choice of newspapers and magazines. Open daily.

▼ AMSTERDAMS HISTORISCH MUSEUM

Condomerie Het Gulden Vlies

Warmoesstraat 141 ⓣ020/627 4174. This shop sells condoms of every shape, size and flavour imaginable. All in the best possible taste – though some items stretch more than the imagination.

Conscious Dreams

Kokopelli Warmoestraat 12 ⓣ020/421 7000, ⓦwww.consciousdreams.nl. One of the first of Amsterdam's so-called "smart shops", with smart drugs, plants, aphrodisiacs, and everything you ever wanted to know about stimulants and maybe more. Very nicely set up, with Internet access and DJs on the weekend. Open till 10pm.

Cyberdog

Spuistraat 250 ⓣ020/330 6385. Amsterdam branch of the club-wear store with a futuristic twist; expect lots of fluorescent clothing, as well as a collection from a few well-known designers. Its in-store box office sells tickets for all club nights from House to Glam Rock.

Delft Shop

Rokin 44 ⓣ020/620 1000, ⓦwww.delftshop.com. Stocks an interesting display of Dutch pottery from small ashtrays and trinkets for €2 to more elaborate designs such as the €7500 replica of a tulip vase held in the Rijksmuseum.

Droog Design

Rusland 3 ⓣ020/626 9809, ⓦwww.droogdesign.nl. Founded in 1993, Droog Design has made a serious contribution to international design – indeed some of their products, such as their milk bottle chandelier, have ended up in museum collections. This is their gallery-cum-shop.

Gallery de Munt

In the Munttoren, Muntplein 12 ⓣ020/623 2271. A good outlet for gifts of antique delftware, pottery, hand-painted tiles and the like.

Jacob Hooij

Kloveniersburgwal 10 ⓣ020/624 3041. Traditional homeopathic chemist with any amount of herbs and natural cosmetics, as well as a huge stock of *drop* (Dutch liquorice); in business at this address since 1778.

Jan Jansen

Rokin 42 ⓣ020/625 1350. Famous Dutch designer selling hand-made shoes with sparky designs.

P.G.C. Hajenius

Rokin 92 ⓣ020/623 7494. Open Sun. Old, established tobacconist selling its own and other brands of cigars, tobacco, smoking accessories, and every make of cigarette you can think of.

Posthumus

Sint Luciensteeg 23 ⓣ020/625 5812. Posh stationery, cards and, best of all, a choice of hundreds of rubber stamps. By appointment to Her Majesty.

De Slegte

Kalverstraat 48 ⓣ020/622 5933. The Amsterdam branch of a nation-wide chain specializing in new and used books at a discount.

Vrolijk

Paleisstraat 135 ⓣ020/623 5142, ⓦwww.vrolijk.nu. The self-proclaimed largest gay and lesbian bookshop in Europe, with books, magazines, videos and more.

Waterstone's

Kalverstraat 152 ⓣ020/638 3821. Amsterdam branch of the UK

high-street chain, with four floors of books and magazines. A predictable selection, but prices are sometimes cheaper here than elsewhere.

Coffeeshops

Abraxas

Jonge Roelensteeg 12. Quirky, mezzanine coffeeshop with challenging spiral staircases, especially afterwards. The hot chocolate with hash is not for the susceptible.

Dampkring

Handboogstraat 29. Colourful coffeeshop and laid-back atmosphere, known for its good-quality hash.

Extase

Oude Hoogstraat 2. Part of a chain run by the initiator of the Hash Museum (see p.76). Considerably less chi-chi than the better-known coffeeshops.

Grasshopper

Oudebrugsteeg 16; Nieuwezijds Voorburgwal 57. Multi-levelled coffeeshop, with bar, sports screen and restaurant. One of the city's more welcoming places, though its proximity to Centraal Station means that at times it can be overwhelmed by tourists.

Homegrown Fantasy

Nieuwezijds Voorburgwal 87a. Attached to the Dutch Passion seed company, this sells the widest selection of marijuana in Amsterdam, most of it local.

Rusland

Rusland 16. One of the first Amsterdam coffeeshops, a cramped but vibrant place that's a favourite with both dope fans and tea addicts (it has 43 different kinds). A cut above the rest.

▼ HOMEGROWN FANTASY

Cafés and tearooms

Arnots

Singel 441. Closed Sat & Sun. A basement café serving some of the best coffee in town along with wholemeal sandwiches and freshly squeezed apples. A great summertime spot with people spilling out onto the pavement.

't Nieuwe Kafe

Eggerstraat 8. Beside the Nieuwe Kerk, this smart bistro-style café is popular with shoppers, serving good, reasonably priced lunches and light meals. Great pancakes too.

Puccini

Staalstraat 21. Lovely cake and chocolate shop-cum-café.

Villa Zeezicht

Torensteeg 3. Excellent rolls and sandwiches, plus some of the best apple cake in the city.

Vlaamse Friethuis

Voetboogstraat 33. The best frites in town – take-out only.

Restaurants

Bern

Nieuwmarkt 9. Casual and inexpensive brown café patronized by a predominantly arty clientele. Run by a native of Switzerland, its speciality is, not surprisingly, excellent and alcoholic cheese fondue.

Centra

Lange Niezel 29 ☎020/622 3050. Daily 1–11pm. Cantina with a wonderful selection of Spanish food, masterfully cooked and genially served.

De Compagnon

Guldehandsteeg 17, via Warmoesstraat ☎020/620 4225. Closed Sun. This restaurant tends to be fully booked well in advance, but you might get in for lunch. With its split-level wooden floors it has an intimate, old Amsterdam atmosphere, traditional food and a wine menu with a choice of 300 bottles.

Green Planet

Spuistraat 122 ☎020/625 8280. Daily 5.30pm–midnight. Cute mezzanine café with lots of tofu dishes and a varied international menu. Cash only.

Hemelse Modder

Oude Waal 9 ☎020/624 3203. Closed Mon. Tasty meat, fish and vegetarian food in French-Italian style at reasonable prices in an informal atmosphere. Highly popular (especially with gay people).

▼ CAFÉ BERN

▲ HOI TIN

Hoi Tin

Zeedijk 122 ☎020/625 6451. Daily noon–midnight. One of the best options in Amsterdam's rather dodgy Chinatown, this is a constantly busy place with an enormous menu (in English too) including some vegetarian dishes.

Kinderkoekcafé

OZ Achterburgwal 193 ☎020/625 3257. Simple food, well done, in a restaurant entirely staffed by children. Only open for weekend diners; the rest of the time they run cookery courses for kids.

Lana Thai

Warmoesstraat 10 ☎020/624 2179. Closed Tues. Among the best Thai restaurants in town, with seating overlooking the water of Damrak. Quality food, chic surroundings but high prices.

Luden

Spuistraat 304 ☎020/622 8979. Excellent French bistro-cum-restaurant that does fine-value *prix fixe* menus, for which you can expect to pay €26.50 for three courses, as well as a more moderately priced *à la carte* menu and brasserie.

Sie Joe

Gravenstraat 24 ☎020/624 1830. Mon–Sat 11am–7pm, Thurs till 8pm. Small Indonesian café-restaurant whose great value-for-money menu is far from extensive but comprises well-prepared, simple dishes such as *gado gado*, *sateh* and *rendang*.

De Silveren Spiegel

Kattengat 4 ☎020/624 6589. Closed Sun. There's been a restaurant in this location since 1614, and "The Silver Mirror" is one of the best in the city, with a delicately balanced menu of Dutch cuisine. The proprietor lives on the coast and brings in the fish himself. Spectacular food, with a cellar of 350 wines to complement it.

Supper Club

Jonge Roelensteeg 21 ☎020/344 6400, ⓦwww.supperclub.nl. A five-course set menu served to cus-

▲ DE SILVEREN SPIEGEL

tomers, who lounge on mattresses, smoking joints and listening to a DJ on a raised stage. The fusion food is of a very high standard, though some may find the whole concept pretentious or downright disconcerting. Customers have free entry to the members-only club downstairs. Booking essential. Expensive.

Vijff Vlieghen

Spuistraat 294 ☎020/530 4060. This immaculate restaurant – one of the city's best – serves exquisitely prepared Dutch (and beyond) food in antique, wood-panelled premises. Hard to beat, but it's expensive.

Bars

Absinthe Bar

Nieuwezijds Voorburgwal 171. Daily 10pm–4am. Small, late-night basement lounge bar, slightly hidden from the street that specializes in – you guessed it – absinthe. Free entry, DJ at weekends.

Belgique

Gravenstraat 2. Tiny and very appealing bar behind the Nieuwe Kerk that serves up Belgian brews.

Blincker

St Barberentraat 7. Hi-tech theatre bar just out of the Red Light District.

De Buurvrouw

St Pieterspoortsteeg 29. Daily from 9pm. Dark, noisy bar with a wildly eclectic crowd; a great alternative place to head for in the centre. Live music on Sun.

Café de Zeemeeuw

Zeedijk 102. Popular, convivial Dutch bar with large sports-screen, just off Nieuwmarkt.

Dantzig

Zwanenburgwal 15. Easy-going grand café, right on and across the water from Waterlooplein. Comfortable chairs, friendly service and a low-key, chic atmosphere. Food served at lunchtime and in the evenings.

De Drie Fleschjes

Gravenstraat 18. Closes 8.30pm. Tasting house for spirits and liqueurs, which once would have been made on the premises. Clients tend to be well heeled or well soused (often both).

De Engelbewaarder

Kloveniersburgwal 59. Once the meeting place of Amsterdam's bookish types, this is still known as a literary café. It's relaxed and informal, with live jazz on Sunday afternoons.

Gollem

Raamsteeg 4. Small and intimate bar with a superb selection of Belgian beers – and with the correct glasses to drink them from. The genial barman will help you choose.

Het Doktertje

Roozenboomsteeg 4. Tiny, dark, brown café with stained glass to keep you hidden from the world outside. Liqueurs fill the wall behind the tiny bar. A place to be enchanted.

▼ DANTZIG

Hoppe

Spui 18. One of Amsterdam's longest-established and best-known bars, and one of its most likeable, frequented by the city's businessfolk on their wayward way home. Summer is especially good, when the throngs spill out onto the street.

De Jaren

Nieuwe Doelenstraat 20. One of the grandest of the grand cafés, overlooking the Amstel next to the university, with three floors, two terraces and a cool, light feel. A great place to nurse the Sunday papers – unusually you'll find English ones here. Reasonably priced food too, and a great salad bar.

Lokaal 't Loosje

Nieuwmarkt 32. Quiet old-style brown café that's been here for two hundred years and looks it. Wonderful for late breakfasts and pensive afternoons.

Luxembourg

Spui 22. The prime watering hole of Amsterdam's advertising and media brigade. If you can get past the crowds, it's actually a long and deep bar with a good selection of snacks, and possibly the best hamburgers in town.

De Twentsche Club

Gravenstraat 10, ⓦwww.detwentscheclub.nl. Thurs–Sun from 4pm. Roomy bar behind the Nieuwe Kerk that has a comfortable back room and a good programme of live jazz. The fortnightly Thursday film club offers an eclectic choice of movies and a three-course meal for €25. Above all, though, it's the authentic nineteenth-century surroundings that appeal – little has changed, even down to the cash register.

Van Kerkwijk

Nes 41. On a thin, theatre-packed alley behind the Dam, this is a highly recommended bar. Wine comes in carafes filled from the barrel, along with a wide choice of cheeses and tasty meals to help it on its way.

Wynand Fockink

Pijlsteeg 31. Small and cosy bar hidden just behind Dam square. One of the older *proeflokalen*. Popular with local street musicians.

Gay bars

Argos

Warmoesstraat 95. From 10pm. Europe's oldest leather bar, with two bars and a raunchy cellar. Not for the weak-kneed.

Cuckoo's Nest

Nieuwezijds Kolk 6. From 1pm. A cruisey leather bar with a long reputation, this is described as "the best place in town for chance encounters". Vast and infamous darkroom.

Why Not

Nieuwezijds Voorburgwal 28, ⓦwww.whynot.nl. Live shows Thurs–Sat. Long-standing, intimate bar and club with a porno cinema above; happy hour 7–9pm.

Clubs and venues

Akhnaton

Nieuwezijds Kolk 25 ⓣ020/624 3396, ⓦwww.akhnaton.nl. A "Centre for World Culture", specializing in African and Latin American music and dance parties. On a good night, the place heaves with people.

Bimhuis

Oude Schans 73–77 ⓣ020/623 1361, ⓦwww.bimhuis.nl. The city's premier jazz venue for almost 28 years, with an excellent auditorium and ultramodern bar. Concerts Thurs–Sat, free sessions Mon–Wed. There's also free live music in the bar on Sun at 4pm. Concert tickets are for sale on the day only.

Dansen bij Jansen

Handboogstraat 11 ⓣ020/620 1779, ⓦwww.dansenbijjansen.nl. Daily 11pm–4am, Sat & Sun till 5am. €2 Sun–Wed, €4 Thurs–Sat, officially you need student ID to get in. Founded by – and for – students, and very popular. Plays a mixture of pop, chart and R&B.

Waalse Kerk

OZ Achterburgwal 157 ⓣ020/236 2236. Weekend and afternoon concerts of early- and chamber music – very soothing.

The Grachtengordel

Medieval Amsterdam was enclosed by the Singel, part of the city's protective moat, but this is now just the first of five canals that reach right around the city centre, extending anticlockwise from Brouwersgracht to the River Amstel in a "girdle of canals" or Grachtengordel. This is without doubt the most charming part of the city, its lattice of olive-green waterways and dinky humpback bridges overlooked by street upon street of handsome seventeenth-century canal houses, almost invariably undisturbed by later development. It's a subtle cityscape – full of surprises, with a bizarre carving here, an unusual facade stone (used to denote name and occupation) there. Architectural peculiarities aside, it is perhaps the district's overall atmosphere that appeals rather than any specific sight. This chapter covers the southern sweep of the Grachtengordel from Raadhuisstraat to the Amstel. The western part – including the Anne Frankhuis – is covered in the following chapter, along with the Jordaan and western dock areas. There's no obvious walking route around the Grachtengordel, indeed you may prefer to wander around as the mood takes you, but the description we've given below goes from north to south, taking in all the highlights on the way. On all three of the main canals, street numbers begin in the north and increase as you go south.

Westermarkt to Leidsegracht

Between Westermarkt and Leidsegracht, the main canals are intercepted by a trio of cross-streets, which are themselves divided into shorter streets, mostly named after animals whose pelts were once used in the local tanning industry. There's Reestraat (Deer Street), Hartenstraat (Hart), Berenstraat (Bear) and Wolvenstraat (Wolf), not to mention Huidenstraat (Street of Hides) and Runstraat – a "run" being a bark used in tanning. The tanners are long gone and today these are eminently appealing shopping

▼ BROUWERSGRACHT WAREHOUSES

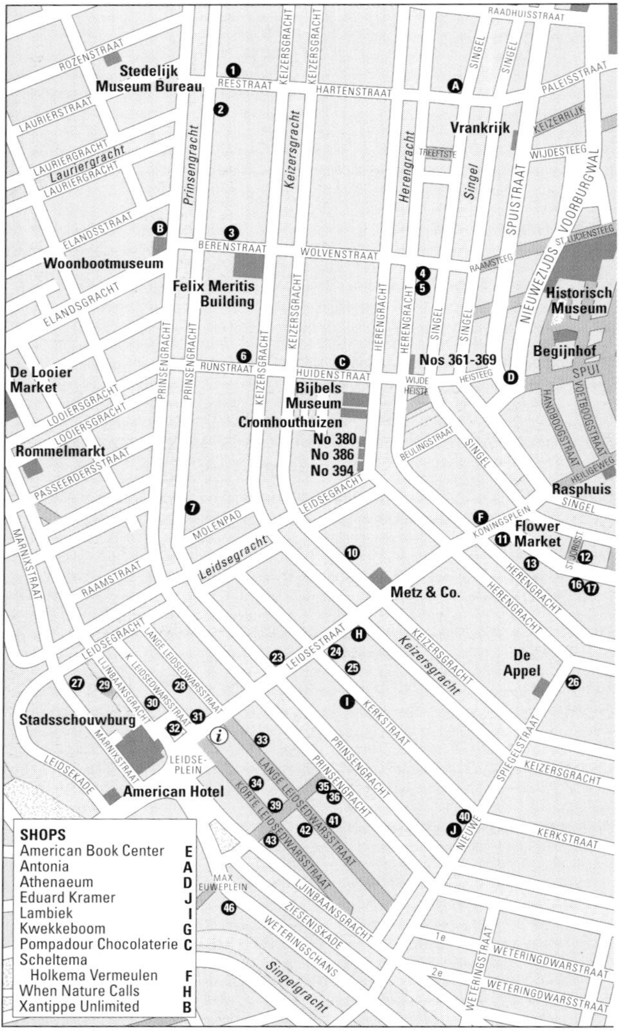

streets, where you can buy everything from carpets to handmade chocolates, toothbrushes to beeswax candles.

The Woonbootmuseum

Prinsengracht 296. March–Oct Wed–Sun 11am–5pm; Nov–Feb Sat–Sun 11am–5pm. €3. This 1914 Dutch houseboat doubles as a tourist attraction with a handful of explanatory plaques about life on the water. Some 3000 barges and houseboats are connected to the city's gas and electricity networks. They are regularly

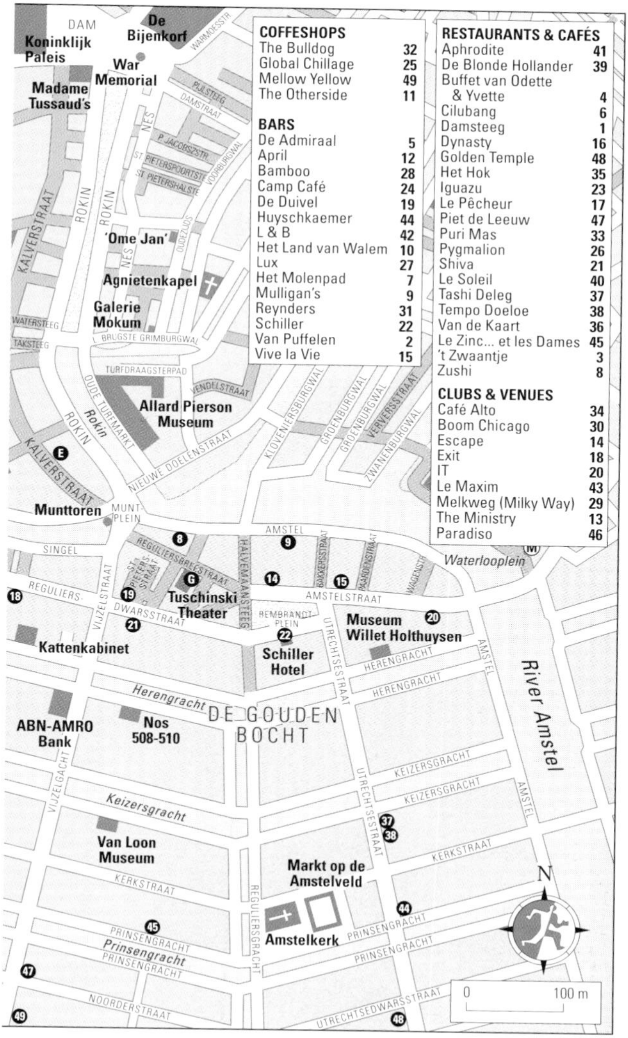

inspected and strict controls ensure their numbers don't proliferate.

The Felix Meritis Building

Keizersgracht 324. A Neoclassical monolith of 1787, this mansion was built to house the artistic and scientific activities of the eponymous society, which was the cultural focus of the city's upper crust for nearly a hundred years. Dutch cultural aspirations did not, however, impress everyone. It's said that when Napoleon visited the city the

The canals

The **canals of the Grachtengordel** were dug in the seventeenth century as part of a comprehensive plan to extend the boundaries of a city no longer able to accommodate its burgeoning population. Increasing the area of the city from two to seven square kilometres was a monumental task, and the conditions imposed by the council were strict. The three main waterways – Herengracht, Keizersgracht and Prinsengracht – were set aside for the residences and businesses of the richer and more influential Amsterdam merchants, while the radial cross-streets were reserved for more modest artisans' homes; meanwhile, immigrants, newly arrived to cash in on Amsterdam's booming economy, were assigned, albeit informally, the Jodenhoek (see p.115) and the Jordaan (see p.107). In the Grachtengordel, everyone, even the wealthiest merchant, had to comply with a set of strict and detailed planning regulations. In particular, the council prescribed the size of each building plot – the frontage was set at thirty feet, the depth two hundred – and although there was a degree of tinkering, the end result was the loose conformity you can see today: tall, narrow residences, whose individualism is mainly restricted to the stylistic permutations amongst the gables.

The earliest extant **gables**, dating from the early seventeenth century, are crow-stepped gables, but these were largely superseded from the 1650s onwards by neck gables and bell gables. Some are embellished, others aren't, many have decorative cornices, some don't, and the fanciest, which almost invariably date from the eighteenth century, sport full-scale balustrades. The plainest gables are those of former **warehouses**, where the deep-arched and shuttered windows line up to either side of loft doors, which were once used for loading and unloading goods, winched by pulley from the street down below. Indeed, outside **pulleys** remain a common feature of houses and warehouses alike, and are often still in use as the easiest way of moving furniture into the city's myriad apartments.

▼ HERENGRACHT HOUSE

entire building was redecorated for his reception, only to have him stalk out in disgust, claiming that the place stank of tobacco. Oddly enough, it later became the headquarters of the Dutch Communist Party, but they sold it to the council who now lease it to the Felix Meritis Foundation for experimental and avant-garde art workshops, discussions and debates.

The Bijbels Museum

Herengracht 366–368 Ⓦ www.bijbelsmuseum.nl. Mon–Sat 10am–5pm, Sun 11am–5pm. €6.
The graceful and commanding Cromhouthuizen, at Herengracht 364–370, consists of four matching stone man-

sions, frilled with tendrils, carved fruit and scrollwork, and graced by dinky little bull's-eye windows and elegant gables. They were built in the 1660s for one of Amsterdam's wealthy merchant families, the Cromhouts, and two of them now house the Bijbels Museum. This contains a thorough selection of Bibles, including the first Dutch-language Bible ever printed, dating from 1477, and a series of idiosyncratic models of Solomon's Temple and the Jewish Tabernacle plus a scattering of archeological finds from Palestine and Egypt.

Leidseplein

Lying on the edge of the Grachtengordel, Leidseplein is the bustling hub of Amsterdam's nightlife, a rather cluttered and disorderly open space that has never had much character. The square once marked the end of the road in from Leiden and, as horse-drawn traffic was banned from the centre long ago, it was here that the Dutch left their horses and carts – a sort of equine car park. Today, it's quite the opposite: continual traffic made up of trams, bikes, cars and pedestrians gives the place a frenetic feel, and the surrounding side streets are jammed with bars, restaurants and clubs in a bright jumble of jutting signs and neon lights. On a good night, however, Leidseplein can be Amsterdam at its carefree, exuberant best.

Stadsschouwburg

Leidseplein www.stadschouwburgamsterdam.nl.

Leidseplein holds one building of architectural note, the grandiose Stadsschouwburg, a neo-Renaissance edifice dating from 1894 which was so widely criticized for its clumsy vulgarity that the city council of the day temporarily withheld the money for decorating the exterior. Home to the National Ballet and Opera until the Muziektheater (see p.175) was completed on Waterlooplein in 1986, it is now used for theatre, dance and music performances, as well as hosting visiting English-language theatre companies. However, its most popular function is as the place where the Ajax football team gather on the balcony to wave to the crowds whenever they win anything – as they often do.

▼ LEIDSEPLEIN

The American Hotel

Leidsekade 97. Just off the square, the American Hotel is one of the city's oddest buildings, a monumental and slightly disconcerting rendering of Art Nouveau, with angular turrets, chunky dormer windows and fancy brickwork. Completed in 1902, the present structure takes its name from its demolished predecessor, which was decorated with statues and murals of North American scenes. Inside the present hotel is the *Café Americain*, once the fashionable haunt of Amsterdam's literati, but now a mainstream location for coffee and lunch. The Art Nouveau decor is well worth a peek – an artful combination of stained glass, shallow arches and geometric patterned brickwork.

▼ AMERICAN HOTEL

▲ METZ & CO ROOFTOP CAFÉ

Leidsestraat to Metz & Co

Heading northeast from Leidseplein, Leidsestraat is a crowded shopping street, a long, slender gauntlet of fashion and shoe shops of little distinction that leads across the girdle of canals up towards the Singel and the Flower Market (see p.96). En route, at the corner of Keizersgracht, is Metz & Co (see p.96). At the time of its construction, this was the tallest commercial building in the city – one reason why the owners were able to entice Gerrit Rietveld, the leading architectural light of the De Stijl movement, to add a rooftop glass and metal showroom in 1933. The showroom has survived and has been turned into a café offering one of the best views over the centre in this predominantly low-rise city.

The Spiegelkwartier

One block east of Metz & Co, along Keizersgracht, is Nieuwe Spiegelstraat, an appealing mixture of bookshops and corner cafés that extends south into Spiegelstraat to form the Spiegelkwartier – home to the pricey end of Amsterdam's antiques trade and well worth an idle wander. While you're here look in on **De Appel**, a lively centre for contemporary art at Nieuwe Spiegelstraat 10 (Tues–Sun 11am–6pm; €2.50, Ⓦwww.deappel.nl).

De Gouden Bocht

Nieuwe Spiegelstraat meets the elegant sweep of Herengracht near the west end of the so-called De Gouden Bocht (Golden Bend), where the canal is overlooked by a long sequence of double-fronted mansions that are some of the most opulent dwellings in the city. Most of the houses here were extensively remodelled in the late seventeenth and eighteenth centuries. Characteristically, they have double stairways leading to the entrance, underneath which the small door was for the servants, whilst up above the majority are topped off by the ornamental cornices that were fashionable at the time. Classical references are common, both in form – pediments, columns and pilasters – and decoration, from scrolls and vases through to geometric patterns inspired by ancient Greece.

The Museum Willet-Holthuysen

Herengracht 605. Mon–Fri 10am–5pm, Sat & Sun 11am–5pm. €4. This museum is billed as "a peep behind the curtains into an historic Amsterdam canal house", which just about sums it up. The house itself dates from 1685, but the interior was remodelled by successive members of the coal-trading Holthuysen family until the last of the line, Sandra Willet-Holthuysen, gifted her home and its contents to the city in 1895. Renovated a number of years ago, most of the public rooms, notably the Blue Room and the Dining Room, have now been returned to their original eighteenth-century Rococo appearance – a flashy and ornate style that the Dutch merchants held to be the epitome of refinement and good taste. At the back of the house are the formal gardens, a neat pattern of miniature hedges graced by the occasional stone statue. There's a small collection of glass, silver, majolica and ceramics in the basement.

▼ MUSEUM WILLET-HOLTHUYSEN

▲ THE BLUE ROOM, MUSEUM WILLET-HOLTHUYSEN

The Amstel and the Magere Brug

The Grachtengordel comes to an abrupt halt at the River Amstel, long the main route into the city, with goods arriving by barge and boat to be traded for the imported materials held in Amsterdam's many warehouses. The Magere Brug (Skinny Bridge) is the most famous and arguably the cutest of the city's many swing bridges. Legend has it that this bridge, which dates back to about 1670, replaced an even older and skinnier version, originally built by two sisters who lived on either side of the river and were fed up with having to walk so far to see each other.

The Amstel Sluizen

The Amstel Sluizen – or Amstel locks – are closed every night when the authorities begin the process of sluicing out the canals. A huge pumping station on an island out to the east of the city then starts to pump fresh water from the IJsselmeer into the canal system; similar locks on the west side of the city are left open for the surplus to flow into the IJ and, from there, out to sea. The watery content of the canals is thus refreshed every three nights – though, despite this, and with three centuries of algae, prams, shopping trolleys and a few hundred rusty bikes, the water remains only appealing as long as you're not actually in it.

The Amstelveld, Amstelkerk and Reguliersgracht

Doubling back from the Amstel sluizen, turn left along the north side of Prinsengracht and you soon reach the small open space of the Amstelveld, an oasis of calm that rarely sees visitors, with the plain seventeenth-century white wooden Amstelkerk occupying one of its corners.

▼ MAGERE BRUG

The Monday market here sells flowers and plants, and is much less of a scrum than the Bloemenmarkt, with lots of friendly advice on what to buy. It's here also that Prinsengracht intersects with Reguliersgracht, probably the prettiest of the three surviving radial canals that cut across the Grachtengordel – its dainty humpback bridges and greening waters overlooked by charming seventeenth- and eighteenth-century canal houses.

▲ AMSTELVELD

Museum Van Loon

Keizersgracht 672. Fri–Mon 11am–5pm. €4.50. The Museum Van Loon boasts the finest accessible canal house interior in Amsterdam. Built in 1672, and first occupied by the artist and pupil of Rembrandt, Ferdinand Bol, the house has been returned to something akin to its eighteenth-century appearance, with acres of wood panelling and fancy stucco work. Look out also for the ornate copper balustrade on the staircase, into which is worked the name "Van Hagen-Trip" (after a one-time owner of the house); the Van Loons later filled the spaces between the letters with fresh iron curlicues to prevent their children falling through. The top-floor landing has several pleasant paintings sporting Roman figures and one of the bedrooms – the "painted room" – is decorated with a Romantic painting of Italy – a favourite motif in Amsterdam from around 1750 to 1820. The oddest items are the fake bedroom doors: the eighteenth-century owners were so keen to avoid any lack of symmetry that they camouflaged the real bedroom doors and created imitation, decorative doors in the "correct" position instead.

Rembrandtplein

One of the larger open spaces in the city centre, Rembrandtplein is a dishevelled bit of greenery that was formerly Amsterdam's butter market. It was renamed in 1876, and is today one of the city's nightlife centres, although its crowded restaurants and bars are firmly tourist-targeted. Rembrandt's statue stands in the middle, his back wisely turned against the square's worst excesses, which include live (but deadly) outdoor muzak. Of the prodigious number of cafés and bars here, only the café of the *Schiller Hotel* at no. 26 stands out, with an original Art Deco interior somewhat reminiscent of an ocean liner.

The Tuschinski

Reguliersbreestraat 26–28. Tucked in among Reguliersbreestraat's slot-machine arcades and sex shops, the Tuschinski is the city's most extraordinary cinema, with a marvellously well-preserved Art Deco interior. Opened in 1921 by a Polish Jew, Abram Tuschinski, the cinema boasts Expressionist paintings, coloured marbles and a wonderful carpet,

▲ MUSEUM VAN LOON

handwoven in Marrakesh to an original design. Tuschinski himself died in Auschwitz in 1942, and there's a plaque in the cinema's foyer in his memory.

The Munttoren and Bloemenmarkt

Tiny Muntplein is dominated by the Munttoren, an imposing fifteenth-century tower that was once part of the old city wall. Later, the tower was adopted as the municipal mint – hence its name – and Hendrik de Keyser, in one of his last commissions, added a flashy spire in 1620. A few metres away, the floating Bloemenmarkt, or flower market (daily 9am–5pm, though some stalls close on Sun), extends along the southern bank of the Singel. Popular with locals and tourists alike, the market is one of the main suppliers of flowers to central Amsterdam, but its blooms and bulbs now share stall space with souvenir clogs, garden gnomes and Delftware.

Shops

American Book Center

Kalverstraat 185 ☎020/625 5537. Bookstore with a vast stock, all in English, with lots of imported US magazines too. Students get ten-percent discount.

Antonia

Gasthuismolensteeg 18 & 6a ☎020/627 2433. A gathering of adventurous Dutch designers, in two male and female locations. Good for shoes and bags.

Athenaeum

Spui 14 ☎020/622 6248. Excellent and browsable all-round bookshop with an adventurous stock – though it's basically a Dutch store. Also the best source of international newspapers and magazines.

Ksisk

Kerkstraat 115. The place to come if you're looking for something unusual to wear.

Eduard Kramer

Nieuwe Spiegelstraat 64 ☎020/623 0832. Antique store with a marvellous selection of fifteenth- to twentieth-century Dutch tiles.

Kwekkeboom

Reguliersbreestraat 36 ☎020/623 1205. One of the city's most famous pastry shops. Also branches at Ferdinand Bolstraat 119 and Linnaeusstraat 80.

Lambiek

Kerkstraat 119 ☎020/626 7543, Ⓦwww.lambiek.nl. The city's largest and oldest comic bookshop and gallery, with an international stock. Their website features the biggest comiclopedia in the world. Due to the rebuilding of their premises, they are temporarily relocated here, but will move back to Kerkstraat 78, just along the street, in due course.

Metz & Co

Keizersgracht 455 ☎020/5207020. A large department store stocking a wide range of designer clothes and occupying a handsome stone building of 1891, complete with caryatids and a fancy corner dome.

Pompadour Chocolaterie

Huidenstraat 12 ⓣ020/623 9554. Chocolates and lots of home-made pastries usually smothered in – or filled with – chocolate.

Scheltema Holkema Vermeulen

Koningsplein 20 ⓣ020/523 1411, ⓦwww.scheltema.nl. Open late and on Sun. Amsterdam's biggest and best bookshop. Six floors of absolutely everything, but mostly in Dutch.

When Nature Calls

Leidsestraat 508 ⓣ020/330 0700. Cannabis and hemp products such as hemp chocolate and beer, plus seeds and magic mushrooms.

Xantippe Unlimited

Prinsengracht 290 ⓣ020/623 5854. Mon 1–7pm, Tues–Fri 10am–7pm, Sat 10am–6pm, Sun 10am–5pm. Amsterdam's foremost women's bookshop, with a wide selection of feminist titles in English.

Zipper

Huidenstraat 7 ⓣ020/623 7302. Great selection of used and vintage clothing.

Coffeeshops

The Bulldog

Leidseplein 15. The biggest and most famous of the coffeeshop chains, and a long way from its pokey Red-Light-District-dive origins. This, the main Leidseplein branch (the Palace), housed in a former police station, has a large cocktail bar, coffeeshop, juice bar and souvenir shop, all with separate entrances. It's big and brash, not at all the place for a quiet smoke, though the dope they sell (packaged up in neat little brand-labelled bags) is reliably good.

Global Chillage

Kerkstraat 51. A celebrated slice of Amsterdam dope culture, always comfortably filled with tie-dyed stone-heads propped up against the walls, so chilled they're horizontal.

Mellow Yellow

Vijzelgracht 33. Sparse but bright coffeeshop with a small but good-quality dope list. A little out of the way, but it makes up for it in friendliness.

The Otherside

Reguliersdwarsstraat 6. Essentially a gay coffeeshop (in Dutch, "the other side" is a euphemism for gay), but heteros are welcome and the atmosphere is relaxed and good fun.

Cafés and tearooms

Buffet van Odette & Yvette

Herengracht 309. Just walking past will get your taste buds going: a serious treat for breakfast or lunch.

Het Hok

Lange Leidsedwarsstraat 134. Games bar, where you can play

▼ HET HOK

backgammon, chess or draughts, or just drink against a backdrop of clicking counters. Pleasingly unpretentious after the plastic restaurants of the rest of the street, though women may find the overwhelmingly male atmosphere off-putting.

Restaurants

Aphrodite

Lange Leidsedwarsstraat 91 ☎020/622 7382. Daily 5pm–midnight. Inexpensive yet refined Greek cooking in a street where you certainly wouldn't expect it. Fair prices too.

De Blauwe Hollander

Leidsekruisstraat 28 ☎020/627 0522. Inexpensive Dutch food in generous quantities – something of a boon in an otherwise touristy, unappealing part of town. Expect to share a table.

Damsteeg

Reestraat 28 ☎020/627 8794. Superb French-inspired cuisine with more than the occasional Dutch gastronomic flourish. In a charmingly renovated old canal house.

Dynasty

Reguliersdwarsstraat 30 ☎020/626 8400. Closed Tues. Festive choice of Indochinese food, with Vietnamese and Thai options: not for the shoestring traveller. The subdued atmosphere suits the prices – main courses average €20–25.

Cilubang

Runstraat 10 ☎020/626 9755. Small Indonesian restaurant, with a friendly atmosphere, serving well-presented, spicy dishes. Moderate prices.

Golden Temple

Utrechtsestraat 126 ☎020/626 8560. Laid-back place with a little more soul than the average Amsterdam veggie joint. Well-prepared, lacto-vegetarian food and pleasant, attentive service. No alcohol and non-smoking throughout.

Iguazu

Prinsengracht 703 ☎020/420 3910. Daily noon–midnight. For carnivores only: a superb, moderately priced Argentinian-Brazilian restaurant, with perhaps the best fillet steak in town.

Le Pêcheur

Reguliersdwarsstraat 32 ☎020/624 3121. Closed Sun. Beautiful restaurant with a well-balanced menu (the four-course set menu is good value at around €35). Lovely garden terrace in the summer. Open for lunch.

Piet de Leeuw

Noorderstraat 11 ☎020/623 7181. Mon–Fri noon–11pm, Sat & Sun 5–11pm. Arguably Amsterdam's best steakhouse, dating from the 1940s, and surprisingly inexpensive. Excellent steaks, and mouthwatering desserts.

Puri Mas

Lange Leidsedwarsstraat 37 ☎020/627 7627. Exceptionally good value for money Indonesian, on a street better known for rip-offs. Friendly and informed service preludes spectacular *rijsttafels*, both meat and vegetarian. Recommended.

Pygmalion

Nieuwe Spiegelstraat 5a ☎020/420 7022. Good spot for both lunch and dinner, popular among locals. South African dishes include crocodile steaks, and there's a good selection of sandwiches and authentic Afrikaner desserts.

Shiva

Reguliersdwarsstraat 72 ⓣ020/624 8713. The city's most outstanding Indian restaurant in terms of quality and price, with a wide selection of dishes, all expertly prepared and moderately priced. Highly recommended.

Le Soleil

Nieuwe Spiegelstraat 56 ⓣ020/622 7147. Open until 6pm. Pretty little restaurant (once visited by the Queen) which makes some great pancakes – try one with ginger and raisins.

Tashi Deleg

Utrechtsestraat 65 ⓣ020/620 6624. Highly recommended Tibetan restaurant, with friendly and accommodating staff dishing up authentic food for around €20 for two courses.

Tempo Doeloe

Utrechtsestraat 75 ⓣ020/625 6718. Reliable, reasonably priced quality place close to Rembrandtplein. As with all Indonesian restaurants, be guided by the waiter when choosing – some of the dishes are very hot indeed.

▼ DE ADMIRAAL

Van de Kaart

Prinsengracht 512 ⓣ020/625 9232. A moderately expensive and very creative restaurant, with an excellent and surprising menu including lobster carpaccio, home-cured bacon and pumpkin-stuffed ravioli. The selection of wines complements the tastes created in the kitchen with vim and gusto.

Le Zinc ... et les Dames

Prinsengracht 999 ⓣ020/622 9044. Closed Sun. Wonderfully atmospheric little place serving good-quality, simple fare with main courses averaging €20–25; there's a particularly good wine list.

't Zwaantje

Berenstraat 12 ⓣ020/623 2373. Old-fashioned Dutch restaurant with a nice atmosphere and well-cooked, reasonably priced food. Well known for its liver and onions.

Zushi

Amstel 20 ⓣ020/330 6882. Daily noon–midnight. High-tech sushi bar, serving colour-coded dishes on a conveyor belt running along the bar.

Bars

De Admiraal

Herengracht 319. Large and uniquely comfortable *proeflokaal*, with a vast range of liqueurs and spirits to explore.

Bamboo

Lange Leidsedwarsstraat 66. Legend has it Chet Baker used to live upstairs and jam on stage to pay his rent. These days the *Bamboo* is an unpretentious, friendly bar playing Seventies and Eighties music. Open from 9pm.

De Duivel

Reguliersdwarsstraat 87. Tucked away on a street of bars and coffeeshops, this is one of the few hip-hop cafés in Amsterdam, with continuous beats and a clientele to match. From 8pm.

Huyschkaemer

Utrechtsestraat 137. Attractive, small, local bar-restaurant on a street renowned for its eateries: a favourite watering hole for arty students. At weekends the restaurant area is turned into a dance floor.

L & B

Korte Leidsedwarsstraat 82. Open until 3am. A cosy bar, rather misplaced among the touristy restaurants and clubs of this part of town. Has a selection of two hundred different whiskies and bourbons.

Het Land van Walem

Keizersgracht 449. A chic bar-café – cool, light, and vehemently un-brown. The clientele is stylish, and the food is a kind of hybrid French-Dutch; there's also a wide selection of newspapers and magazines, including some in English. Breakfast in the garden during the summer is a highlight. Usually packed.

Lux

Marnixstraat 403. Open late. The most trendy option among this stretch of cafés, drawing a young alternative crowd. Loud music.

Het Molenpad

Prinsengracht 653. This is one of the most appealing brown cafés in the city – a long, dark bar that also serves remarkably good food. Fills up with a young, professional crowd after 6pm. Recommended.

Morlang

Keizersgracht 451. Occasional live music and decent food in this new-wave designer bar.

Mulligan's

Amstel 100. By far the best Irish pub in the city, with an authentic atmosphere, Gaelic music and good service.

▼ SCHILLER

Schiller

Rembrandtplein 26. Art Deco bar of the hotel upstairs, authentic in both feel and decor, and offering a genteel escape from the tackiness of much of the Rembrantplein.

Van Puffelen

Prinsengracht 377. A bar and restaurant adjacent to each other. The café is an appealing place to drink, with a huge choice of international beers and a reading room; the restaurant (daily 6–11pm) serves French food, which, though not cheap, is usually well worth it.

▲ VAN PUFFELEN

Reynders

Leidseplein 6. The last real option if you want to sit out on the Leidseplein. A remnant of days long gone, with aproned waiters and an elegant interior.

Gay bars

April

Reguliersdwarsstraat 37. On the itinerary of almost every gay visitor to Amsterdam. Lively and cosmopolitan, with a good selection of foreign newspapers, cakes and coffee, as well as booze.

Camp Café

Kerkstraat 45. Pleasant mix of friendly regulars and foreign visitors. Worth a visit for the ceiling alone, which is covered with a collection of beer mugs from around the world.

Vive la Vie

Amstelstraat 7. Small, campy bar, patronized mostly, but not exclusively, by women and transvestites.

Clubs and venues

Café Alto

Korte Leidsedwarsstraat 115 ⓣ020/626 3249, ⓦwww.jazz-café-alto.nl. It's worth hunting out this legendary little jazz bar just off Leidseplein for its quality modern jazz, performed every night from 10pm until 3am (and often much later). It's big on atmosphere, though slightly cramped, and entry is free.

Boom Chicago

Korte Leidsedwarsstraat 12 ⓣ020/530 7300, ⓦwww.boomchicago.nl. Something of a phenomenon in Amsterdam in recent years, this rapid-fire improv comedy troupe performs nightly to crowds of both tourists and locals, and has received rave reviews from *Rough Guide* readers, the Dutch and international press alike. With inexpensive food, the cheapest beer in town, and a Smoke Boat Cruise following most shows at 10.30pm, the comedy need not be funny – but it is.

Carré Theatre

Amstel 115–125 ⓣ0900/252 5255, ⓦwww.theatercarre.nl. A splendid hundred-year-old structure (originally built for a circus) which represents the ultimate venue for Dutch folk artists, and hosts all kinds of top international acts: anything from Russian folk dance to *La Cage aux Folles*, with reputable touring orchestras and opera companies squeezed in between.

Circustheater Elleboog

Passeerdersgracht 32 ⓣ 020/623 5326, ⓦ www.elleboog.nl. Kids can learn to juggle, be a clown and practise face-painting here – all for €20.

Escape

Rembrandtplein 11 ⓣ 020/622 1111, ⓦ www.escape.nl. What once used to be a cheesy disco is now home to one of Amsterdam's hottest Saturday nights, "Chemistry", with regular appearances by top DJs. A vast place, with room for 2000 people (although you may still have to queue).

Exit

Reguliersdwarsstraat 37 ⓣ 020/625 8788. Free. A classic gay club in the centre of town. Current sounds play nightly to an upbeat, cruisy crowd. Predominantly male, though women are admitted.

IT

Amstelstraat 24 ⓣ 020/625 0111, ⓦ www.it.nl. Large disco with a fine sound system that's popular with a mixed gay/straight crowd. Recently refurbished in a cool New York club style and attracting a dressed up, uninhibited clientele.

Korsakoff

Lijnbaansgracht 161 ⓣ 020/625 7854. Free. Late-night performances by some of the better-known local grunge bands, in a lively setting with cheap drinks and a post-punk clientele.

Maloe Melo

Lijnbaansgracht 163 ⓣ 020/420 4592, ⓦ www.maloemelo.nl. Next door to the *Korsakoff*, a dark, low-ceilinged bar, with a small back room featuring lively local blues(y) acts.

Le Maxim

Leidsekruisstraat 35 ⓣ 020/624 1920. Intimate piano bar that's been going since the Sixties, with live music nightly.

Melkweg (Milky Way)

Lijnbaansgracht 234a ⓣ 020/531 8181, ⓦ www.melkweg.nl. Wed–Sun 2–9pm (dinner from 5.30pm). Probably Amsterdam's most famous entertainment venue, and these days one of the city's prime arts centres, with a young, hip clientele. A former dairy (hence the name) just round the corner from Leidseplein, with two separate halls for live music, putting on a broad range of bands covering everything from reggae to rock, all of which lean towards the "alternative". Late on Friday and Saturday nights, excellent disco sessions go on well into the small hours, sometimes featuring the best DJs in town. As well as the gigs, there's also a monthly film programme, a theatre, gallery, and bar and restaurant (Marnixstraat entrance). Concerts start 9–11pm.

The Ministry

Reguliersdwarsstraat 12 ⓣ 020/623 3981. Open late. Quality DJs playing everything from garage and house through to R&B. Monday-night jam session features the local jazz talent.

Paradiso

Weteringschans 6–8 ⓣ 020/626 4521, ⓦ www.paradiso.nl. A converted church near the Leidseplein, with bags of atmosphere, featuring bands ranging from the up-and-coming to the famous – the Rolling Stones once appeared here. It has been known to host classical concerts too, as well as debates and multimedia events. Bands usually get started around 9pm.

The western canals and the Jordaan

The western stretches of the Grachtengordel comprise Amsterdam's most likeable and unpretentious district, with attractions ranging from the low-key lure of picturesque Brouwersgracht to must-see sights like the Anne Frank House. West of Prinsengracht, the Jordaan was never subject to the rigorous planning restrictions of the main *grachten*, its streets following the lines of the original polder drainage ditches rather than any municipal outline. An easily explored area of slender canals and narrow streets flanked by an agreeable mix of modest, modern terraces and handsome seventeenth-century canal houses, its character has been transformed by a middle-class influx, and it has become one of the most sought-after residential neighbourhoods. Until the late 1970s, the inhabitants were primarily stevedores and factory workers, earning a crust in the pint-sized Scheepvaartsbuurt (Shipping Quarter), now a mixed shopping and residential quarter. Just beyond, the Westerdok is the oldest part of the sprawling complex of artificial islands that today sweeps along the south side of the River IJ.

▼ STATUE OF ANNE FRANK

Brouwersgracht

Running east to west along the northern edge of the three main canals is leafy Brouwersgracht, one of the most picturesque waterways in the city. In the seventeenth century, Brouwersgracht lay at the edge of Amsterdam's great harbour. This was where many of the ships returning from the East unloaded their silks and spices, and as one of the major arteries linking the open sea with the city centre, it was lined with storage depots and warehouses. Breweries flourished here too, capitalizing on their ready access to shipments of fresh water. Today, the harbour bustle has moved elsewhere, and the

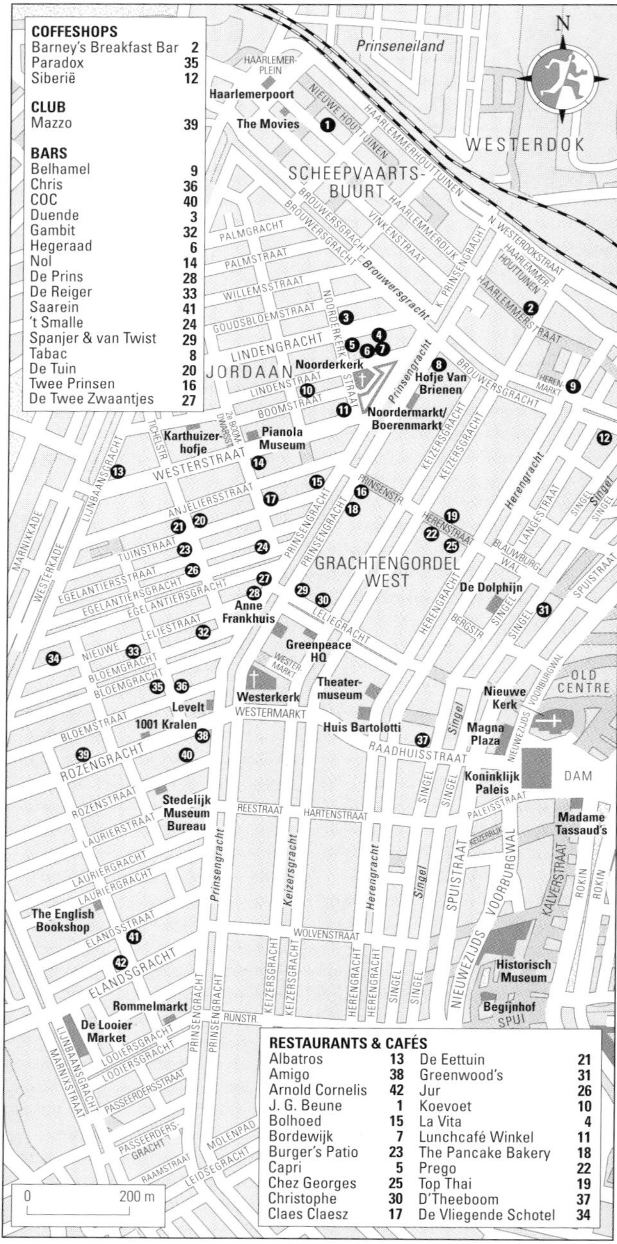
COFFESHOPS
Barney's Breakfast Bar 2
Paradox 35
Siberië 12
CLUB
Mazzo 39
BARS
Belhamel 9
Chris 36
COC 40
Duende 3
Gambit 32
Hegeraad 6
Nol 14
De Prins 28
De Reiger 33
Saarein 41
't Smalle 24
Spanjer & van Twist 29
Tabac 8
De Tuin 20
Twee Prinsen 16
De Twee Zwaantjes 27
RESTAURANTS & CAFÉS
Albatros 13
Amigo 38
Arnold Cornelis 42
J. G. Beune 1
Bolhoed 15
Bordewijk 7
Burger's Patio 23
Capri 5
Chez Georges 25
Christophe 30
Claes Claesz 17
De Eettuin 21
Greenwood's 31
Jur 26
Koevoet 10
La Vita 4
Lunchcafé Winkel 11
The Pancake Bakery 18
Prego 22
Top Thai 19
D'Theeboom 37
De Vliegende Schotel 34
N
Prinseneiland
WESTERDOK
Haarlemerpoort
The Movies
SCHEEPVAARTS-
BUURT
JORDAAN
Noorderkerk
Hofje Van Brienen
Noordermarkt/ Boerenmarkt
Karthuizer-hofje
Pianola Museum
GRACHTENGORDEL WEST
De Dolphijn
Anne Frankhuis
Greenpeace HQ
Westerkerk
Theater-museum
Huis Bartolotti
Nieuwe Kerk
OLD CENTRE
Magna Plaza
Koninklijk Paleis
DAM
Madame Tassaud's
Levelt
1001 Kralen
Stedelijk Museum Bureau
The English Bookshop
Rommelmarkt
De Looier Market
Historisch Museum
Begijnhof
SPUI
WESTERSTRAAT
ROZENGRACHT
LINDENGRACHT
BROUWERSGRACHT
RAADHUISSTRAAT
Prinsengracht
Keizersgracht
Herengracht
Singel
ELANDSGRACHT
LEIDSEGRACHT
0 200 m

warehouses, with their distinctive spout-neck gables and shuttered windows, formerly used for the delivery and dispatch of goods by pulley from the canal below, have been converted into apartments, some of the most expensive in Amsterdam. There are handsome merchants' houses here as well, plus moored houseboats and a string of quaint little swing bridges.

Hofje Van Brienen

Prinsengracht 85–133. Daily 6am–6pm & Sat 6am–2pm. Free. This brown-brick courtyard, originally the site of a brewery, was built as an almshouse in 1804 to the order of Aernout van Brienen. A well-to-do merchant, Brienen had locked himself in his own strong room by accident and, in a panic, he vowed to build a *hofje* if he was rescued. The plaque inside the complex doesn't, however, give much of the game away, inscribed demurely with "for the relief and shelter of those in need."

Leliegracht

Further down Prinsengracht, Leliegracht leads off to the left, one of the tiny radial canals that cut across the Grachtengordel. It holds one of the city's finest Art Nouveau buildings, a tall and striking building at the Leliegracht-Keizersgracht junction designed by Gerrit van Arkel in 1905. Originally the headquarters of a life insurance company – hence the two mosaics with angels recommending policies to bemused earthlings – it's now occupied by Greenpeace.

De Dolphijn

A little further on, over Herengracht on to the Singel, the red-brick and stone-trimmed house at nos 140–142 was once home to Captain Banningh Cocq, the principal soldier in Rembrandt's *Night Watch*.

The Anne Frankhuis

Prinsengracht 263
www.annefrank.nl. Daily: April–Aug 9am–9pm; Sept–March 9am–7pm; closed Yom Kippur. €7.50, 10- to 17-year-olds €3.50, under-10s free.
Easily the city's most visited sight, the Anne Frankhuis is where the young diarist and her family hid from the Germans during World War II. Since the posthumous publication of her diaries, Anne Frank has become extraordinarily famous, in the first instance for recording the iniquities of the Holocaust, and latterly as a symbol of the fight against oppression and in particular racism. The family spent over two years in hiding here, but were eventually betrayed and dispatched to Westerbork – the transit camp in the north of the country where most Dutch Jews were processed before being moved to Belsen or Auschwitz. Of the eight from the annexe, only Otto Frank survived; Anne and her sister died of typhus within a short time of each other in Belsen, just one week before the German surrender.

Anne Frank's diary was among the few things left behind in the annexe. It was retrieved by one of the people who had helped the Franks and handed to Anne's father on his return from Auschwitz; he later decided to publish it. Since its appearance in 1947, it has been constantly in print, translated into over sixty languages, and has sold millions of copies. Despite being so popular, the house has managed to preserve a sense of intimacy, a poignant witness to the personal nature of the Franks' sufferings. The rooms the Franks occupied for two years have been left much the same as they were during the war – even down to the movie star pin-ups in Anne's bedroom and the marks on the wall recording the children's heights. Video clips on the family in particular and the Holocaust in general give the background. Anne Frank was one of about 100,000 Dutch Jews who died during World War II, but this, her final home, provides one of the most enduring testaments to its horrors.

▲ BLOEMGRACHT

The Westerkerk

April–Sept Mon–Fri 11am–3pm. Free.
Trapped in her house, Anne Frank liked to listen to the bells of the Westerkerk, just along Prinsengracht, until they were taken away to be melted down for the German war effort. The church still dominates the district, its 85-metre tower (May–Sept Mon–Sat 10am–5pm; €3) – without question Amsterdam's finest – soaring graciously above its surroundings. On its top perches the crown of Emperor Maximilian, a constantly recurring symbol of Amsterdam and the finishing touch to what was only the second city church to be built expressly for the Protestants. The church was designed by Hendrick de Keyser and completed in 1631 as part of the general enlargement of the city, but whereas the exterior is all studied elegance, the interior is bare and plain. The church is also the reputed resting place of Rembrandt, though the location of his pauper's tomb is not known. Instead, a small memorial in the north aisle commemorates the artist, close to the spot where his son Titus was buried. Rembrandt adored his son – as evidenced by numerous portraits – and the boy's death dealt a final crushing blow to the ageing and embittered artist, who died just over a year later.

Westermarkt

Westermarkt, an open square in the shadow of the Westerkerk, possesses two evocative statues. At the back of the church, beside Keizersgracht, are the three pink granite triangles (one each for the past, present and future) of the **Homo-Monument**. The world's first memorial to persecuted gays and lesbians, commemorating all those who died at the hands of the Nazis, it was designed by Karin Daan and recalls the pink triangles the Germans made homosexuals sew onto their clothes during World War II. Nearby, on the south side of the church by Prinsengracht, is a small but beautifully crafted statue of **Anne Frank** by the modern Dutch sculptor Mari Andriessen – also the creator of the dockworker statue outside Amsterdam's Portuguese Synagogue (see p.120).

The Theatermuseum

Herengracht 168. Tues–Fri 11am–5pm, Sat & Sun 1–5pm. €4.50. A few metres from the Westermarkt, the Theatermuseum holds a moderately enjoyable collection of theatrical bygones, from props through to stage sets, with a particularly good selection of costumes and posters. The museum, which spreads over into the adjoining buildings, also offers a lively programme of temporary exhibitions, but it's the house itself which is of most interest. Dating from 1638, Herengracht 168 has a fetching sandstone facade to a design by Philip Vingboons, arguably the most talented architect involved in the creation of the Grachtengordel. The house was built for Michael de Pauw, a leading light in the East India Company, and the interior sports an extravagant painted ceiling of the Four Seasons by Jacob de Wit plus a splendid spiral staircase.

Huis Bartolotti

Herengracht 170–172. No public access. Next door to the Theatermuseum, the Huis Bartolotti is a tad earlier and a good deal flashier, its pirouetting facade of red-brick and stone dotted with urns and columns, faces and shells. The house is an excellent illustration of the Dutch Renaissance style, and as such is much more ornate than the typical Amsterdam canal house. The architect was Hendrick de Keyser and a director of the West India Company, Willem van den Heuvel, footed the bill. Heuvel inherited a fortune from his Italian uncle and changed his name in his honour to Bartolotti – hence the name of the house.

The Jordaan

According to dyed-in-the-wool locals, the true Jordaaner is born within earshot of the Westerkerk bells, which means that there are endless arguments as to quite where the district's southern boundary lies, though at least the other borders are clear – Prinsengracht, Brouwersgracht and Lijnbaannsgracht. There is also no arguing that the Rozengracht is at the centre of today's Jordaan, though this wide street lost most of its character when its canal was filled in and is now a busy main road of no particular distinction. It was here, at no. 184, that Rembrandt spent the last ten years of his life in diminished circumstances – a scrolled plaque distinguishes his old home.

Rozengracht to Westerstraat

The streets and canals extending north from Rozengracht to Westerstraat form the heart of the Jordaan and hold the district's prettiest sights. Beyond Rozengracht, the first canal is the **Bloemgracht** (Flower Canal), a leafy waterway dotted

▼ BLOEMGRACHT HOUSES

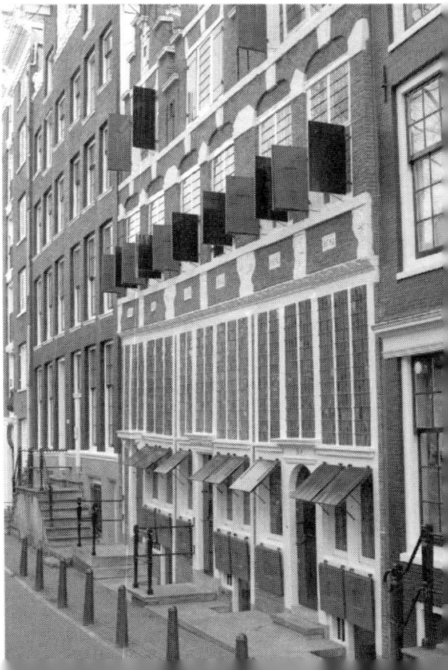

with houseboats and arched by dinky little bridges, its network of cross-streets sprinkled with cafés, bars and idiosyncratic shops. A narrow cross-street – 2e Egelantiersdwarsstraat and its continuation 2e Tuindwarsstraat and 2e Anjeliersdwarsstraat – runs north from Bloemgracht flanked by many of the Jordaan's more fashionable stores and clothing shops as well as some of its liveliest bars and cafés. At the end is workaday **Westerstraat**, a busy modern thoroughfare dotted with more mainstream shops.

▼ PIANOLA MUSEUM

Pianola Museum

Westerstraat 106. Sun 11.30am–5.30pm. €4. The small but fascinating Pianola Museum has a collection of pianolas and automatic music-machines that dates from the beginning of the twentieth century. Fifteen have been restored to working order. These machines, which work on rolls of perforated paper, were the jukeboxes of their day, and the museum has a vast collection of 14,000 rolls of music, some of which were "recorded" by famous pianists and composers – Gershwin, Debussy, Scott Joplin, Art Tatum and others. The museum runs a regular programme of pianola music concerts, where the rolls are played back on the restored machines.

The Noorderkerk

Noordekerkstraat. March–Nov Mon–Sat 10am–4pm. Free.
Noorderkerk is Hendrik de Keyser's last creation and probably his least successful, finished two years after his death in 1623. A bulky, overbearing brick building, it represented a radical departure from the conventional church designs of the time, having a symmetrical Greek-cross floor plan, with four equally proportioned arms radiating out from a steepled centre. Uncompromisingly dour, it proclaimed the serious intent of the Calvinists who worshipped here in so far as the pulpit was at the centre and not at the front of the church, a symbolic break with the Catholic past.

Noordermarkt

The Noordermarkt, the somewhat inconclusive square outside the church, holds a statue of three figures bound to each other, a powerful tribute to the bloody Jordaanoproer riot of 1934, part of a successful campaign to stop the government cutting unemployment benefit during the Depression. The square also hosts some of Amsterdam's best markets – an antiques and general household goods market on Monday mornings (9am–1pm) and the popular farmers' market, the Boerenmarkt, on Saturdays (9am–3pm). Saturday also sees a

▲ NOORDERKERK

bird market (8am–1pm), but caged birds are not everyone's cup of tea.

Lindengracht

The Lindengracht ("Canal of Limes") lost its waterway decades ago, but has had a prominent role in local folklore since the day in 1886 when a policeman made an ill-advised attempt to stop an eel-pulling contest. Horrible as it sounds, eel-pulling was a popular pastime hereabouts with tug-o'-war teams holding tight to either end of the poor creature, which was smeared with soap to make the entertainment last a little longer. The crowd unceremoniously bundled the policeman away, but when reinforcements arrived, the whole thing got out of hand and there was a full-scale riot – the "Paling-Oproer" – which lasted for three days and cost 26 lives.

The Scheepvaartsbuurt and the Westerdok

Brouwersgracht marks both the northern edge of the Jordaan and the southern boundary of the Scheepvaartsbuurt – the Shipping Quarter – an unassuming neighbourhood which focuses on Haarlemmerstraat and Haarlemmerdijk, a long, rather ordinary thoroughfare lined with bars, cafés and food shops. In the eighteenth and nineteenth centuries, this district boomed from its location between the Brouwersgracht and the Westerdok, a narrow parcel of land dredged out of the River IJ immediately to the north and equipped with docks, warehouses and shipyards. The construction of these artificial islands took the pressure off Amsterdam's congested maritime facilities and was necessary to sustain the city's economic success. The Westerdok hung on to some of the marine trade until the 1960s, but today – bar the odd small boatyard – industry has to all intents and purposes disappeared and the area is busy reinventing itself. There is still an air of faded grittiness here, but the old forgotten warehouses – within walking distance of the centre – are rapidly being turned into bijou studios and dozens of plant-filled houseboats are moored along the Westerdok itself and the adjoining Realengracht. Nearby, the Westerpark provides a touch of green, beyond which Het Schip Museum, in the seminal Amsterdam School housing estate of the same name, explores the history of the architectural movement.

▲ NOORDERMARKT STATUE

Shops

Donald E. Jongejans

Noorderkestraat 18 ⊕020/624 6888. Antique spec store that supplied the frames for Bertolucci's The Last Emperor.

Kitsch Kitchen

Bloemdwarsstraat 21 ⊕020/622 8261. Crammed full of bowls, spoons and kitsch stuff in day-glo colours.

Levelt

Prinsengracht 180 ⊕020/624 0823. A specialist tea and coffee company has occupied this shop for over 150 years, and much of the original decor remains, although there are now branches in almost every other part of the city too.

The English Bookshop

Lauriergracht 71 ⊕020/626 4230. A well-chosen collection of titles, many of which you won't find elsewhere.

1001 Kralen

Rozengracht 54 ⊕020/624 3681. "Kralen" means beads, and 1001 would seem a conservative estimate in this place, which sells nothing but.

Coffeeshops

Barney's Breakfast Bar

Haarlemmerstraat 102. Something of an Amsterdam institution, this extremely popular café-cum-coffeeshop is simply the most civilized place in town to enjoy a big joint with a fine breakfast at any time of the day.

Kadinsky

Rosmarijnsteeg 9. Great deals weighed out to a jazz backdrop; great cookies too.

Paradox

1e Bloemdwarsstraat 2. Closes 8pm. If you're fed up with the usual coffeeshop food offerings of burgers, *Paradox* satisfies the munchies with outstanding natural food, including spectacular fresh fruit concoctions.

Siberië

Brouwersgracht 11. Very relaxed, very friendly, and worth a visit whether you want to smoke or not.

Cafés and tearooms

Arnold Cornelis

Elandsgracht 78. Closed Sun. Confectioner with a snug tearoom.

J.G. Beune

Haarlemmerdijk 156 ☎020/624 8356. Handmade cakes and chocolates in an old-style interior. Tearoom attached.

Greenwood's

Singel 103. Small, English-style teashop in the basement of a canal house. Pies and sandwiches, pots of tea – and a decent breakfast.

Lunchcafé Winkel

Noordermarkt 43. Well-weathered neighbourhood café on the corner with Westerstraat that is a popular rendezvous on Saturday and Monday mornings, when the market's in full flow.

Restaurants

Albatros

Westerstraat 264 ☎020/627 9932. Closed Tues & Wed. Family-run restaurant serving some mouth-wateringly imaginative fish dishes. A place to splash out and linger over a meal. Expensive.

Amigo

Rozengracht 5 ☎020/623 1140. Daily except Wed 2–10pm. Basic but good-value Surinamese restaurant close to the Westerkerk.

Bolhoed

Prinsengracht 60 ☎020/626 1803. Daily noon–10pm. Something of an Amsterdam institution. Familiar vegan and vegetarian options from the daily changing menu, with organic beer to wash it down. More expensive than you might imagine.

Bordewijk

Noordermarkt 7 ☎020/624 3899. A chic, expensive restaurant serving stylish French cuisine – a favourite of local food writer Johannes van Dam.

Burger's Patio

2e Tuindwarsstraat 12 ☎020/623 6854. Despite the name (the site used to be occupied by a butcher's), there isn't a burger in sight in this convivial and inexpensive Italian restaurant where you compose your own main course from several given options.

Capri

Lindengracht 61 ☎020/624 4940. Good café-restaurant with much of the joyful atmosphere of the neighbouring market on Saturday. Inexpensive.

Chez Georges

Herenstraat 3 ☎020/626 3332. Closed Wed & Sun. A highly rated, upmarket Belgian eatery, where the emphasis is on meat; main courses €20 and up.

La Vita

Lindengracht 31 ☎020/624 8987. Kitchen closes at 11pm. Authentic Italian-style pizzeria serving

▼ BOLHOED

ridiculously cheap meals. Soups and salads start from €2.75, pizzas and pasta from €3.75.

Christophe

Leliegracht 46 ⓣ020/625 0807. Closed Sun. Classic Michelin-starred restaurant on a quiet and beautiful canal, drawing inspiration from the olive-oil-and-basil flavours of southern France and the chef's early years in North Africa. His aubergine terrine with cumin has been dubbed the best vegetarian dish in the world. Advance reservations essential.

Claes Claesz

Egelantiersstraat 24 ⓣ020/625 5306. Closed Mon. Exceptionally friendly and moderate Jordaan restaurant that attracts a mixed crowd and serves excellent Dutch food. Live music from Thursday to Saturday, and Sunday's "theatre-dinner" sees various Dutch theatrical/musical acts between the courses.

De Eettuin

2e Tuindwarsstraat 10 ⓣ020/623 7706. Hefty and imminently affordable portions of Dutch food, with salad from a serve-yourself bar. Non-meat eaters can content themselves with the large, if dull, vegetarian plate, or the delicious fish casserole.

▼ DE EETTUIN

De Gouden Reael

Zandhoek 14 ⓣ020/623 3883. Mon–Sat from 6pm. Fine French food (€20 per main course and up) in a unique setting up in the Westerdok. The bar, as described in the novel of the same name by Jan Mens, has a long association with the dockworkers.

Jur

Egelantiersgracht 72 ⓣ020/423 4287. Friendly French-Belgian restaurant serving steaks and grilled fare to a wide-ranging clientele. Also has a bar with five draught beers on tap.

Koevoet

Lindenstraat 17 ⓣ020/624 0846. Closed Sun & Mon. The "Cow's-Foot" – or, alternatively, the "Crowbar" – is a traditional Jordaan *eetcafé* serving creative dishes soused with some excellent sauces.

The Pancake Bakery

Prinsengracht 191 ⓣ020/625 1333. Daily noon–9.30pm. Open all day, this place in a beautiful old house on the canal has a large selection of filled pancakes from €6.75. The bigger ones are a meal in themselves.

Prego

Herenstraat 25 ⓣ020/638 0148. Small restaurant serving exceptionally high-quality but pricey Mediterranean cuisine from €30 or so for two courses. Polite and friendly staff.

D'Theeboom

Singel 210 ⓣ020/623 8420. Classic, ungimmicky French cuisine – around €30 for two courses.

Top Thai

Herenstraat 22 ⓣ020/ 623 4633. One of three Top Thai restaurants located around Amsterdam, serving inexpensive, tasty food in healthy portions. The menu gives a handy chilli rating – try the Swimming Hot Beef for total burnout. Cosy atmosphere.

De Vliegende Schotel

Nieuwe Leliestraat 162 ⓣ020/625 2041. Perhaps the pick of the city's cheap and wholesome vegetarian restaurants, the "Flying Saucer" serves delicious food in large portions. Lots of space, a peaceful ambience – and a good notice board.

Bars

Belhamel

Brouwersgracht 60. Kitschy bar/restaurant with an Art Nouveau-style interior and excellent, though costly, French food. The main attraction in summer is one of the prettiest views in Amsterdam.

Chris

Bloemstraat 42. Very proud of itself for being the Jordaan's (and Amsterdam's) oldest bar, dating from 1624. Comfortable, homely atmosphere.

Duende

Lindengracht 62. Wonderful little tapas bar with good, cheap tapas (from around €3) to help your drink go down. Also includes a small venue in the back for live dance and music performances, including regular flamenco.

Gambit

Bloemgracht 20. Chess bar, with boards laid out daily from 1pm until midnight.

Hegeraad

Noordermarkt 34. Lovingly maintained, old-fashioned brown café with a fiercely loyal clientele. The back room, furnished with red plush and paintings, is the perfect place to relax with a hot chocolate.

▼ CHRIS

Nol

Westerstraat 109. Probably the epitome of the jolly Jordaan singing bar, a luridly lit dive that closes late, especially at weekends, when the back-slapping joviality and drunken singalongs keep you rooted until the small hours.

De Prins

Prinsengracht 124. Food served 10am–10pm. Boisterous bar with a wide range of drinks and a well-priced menu. A great place to drink in a nice part of town.

De Reiger

Nieuwe Leliestraat 34. The Jordaan's main meeting place, an old-style café filled with modish Amsterdammers. Affordable good food.

't Smalle

Egelantiersgracht 12. Candle-lit and comfortable, with a barge out front for relaxed summer afternoons. One of Amsterdam's oldest cafés, opened in 1786 as a *proeflokaal* – a tasting house for the (long gone) gin distillery next door.

▼ 'T SMALLE

Spanjer & van Twist

Leliegracht 60. A gentle place, which comes into its own on summer afternoons, with chairs lining one of the most peaceful stretches of water in the city centre.

Tabac

Brouwersgracht 101. Cosy drinking hole on the fringes of the Jordaan (corner of Prinsengracht), which also serves inexpensive Indonesian snacks and light dishes in a convivial atmosphere.

De Tuin

2e Tuindwarsstraat 13. The Jordaan has some marvellously unpretentious bars, and this is one of the best: agreeably unkempt and always filled with locals.

Twee Prinsen

Prinsenstraat 27. Cornerside people-watching bar that's a useful starting place for touring the area. Its heated terrace makes it possible to sit outside even in winter.

De Twee Zwaantjes

Prinsengracht 114. Tiny Jordaan bar whose live accordion music and raucous singing you'll either love or hate. Fun, in an oom-pah-pah sort of way.

Gay bars

COC

Rozenstraat 14 ⓣ020/626 3087, ⓦwww.coc.nl. Successful women-only disco and café, popular with younger lesbians, held every Sat from 8–10pm and called "Just Girls". Pumping on Friday nights too, but then it's mixed men and women. COC is the headquarters of the Netherlands' national gay organization.

Saarein

Elandsstraat 119 ⓣ020/623 4901. Closed Mon. Known for years for its stringent women-only policy, *Saarein* has now opened its doors to men. Though some of the former glory of this café is gone, it's still a warm, relaxing place to take it easy, with a cheerful atmosphere. Also a useful starting point for contacts and information.

Clubs and venues

Mazzo

Rozengracht 114 ⓣ020/626 7500, ⓦwww.mazzo.nl. Open Thurs–Sun. 23yrs+ only. One of the city's hippest clubs, with a choice of music to appeal to all tastes. Perhaps the easiest-going bouncers in town.

The Old Jewish Quarter and Eastern Docks

Originally one of the marshiest parts of Amsterdam, the narrow slice of land sandwiched between the curve of the River Amstel, Kloveniersburgwal and the Nieuwe Herengracht was the home of Amsterdam's Jews from the sixteenth century up until World War II. By the 1920s, this Old Jewish Quarter, aka the Jodenhoek ("Jews' Corner"), was one of the busiest parts of town, crowded with tenement buildings and smoking factories, its main streets holding scores of open-air stalls selling everything from pickled herrings to pots and pans. The war put paid to all this and in 1945 it lay derelict. Postwar redevelopment has not treated it kindly. New building has robbed the district of much of its character and its focal point, Waterlooplein, has been overwhelmed by a whopping town and concert hall complex, which caused much controversy. The once-bustling Jodenbreestraat is now bleak and very ordinary, with Mr Visserplein, at its east end, one of the city's busiest traffic junctions. Picking your way round these obstacles is not much fun, but persevere – amongst the cars and concrete are several moving reminders of the Jewish community that perished in the war. Next door is the Plantagebuurt, a well-to-do residential area that's home to the Artis Zoo and the excellent Verzetsmuseum (Dutch Resistance Museum), and from here it's a short hop north to the reclaimed islands of the Oosterdok, where pride of place goes to the Nederlands Scheepvaartmuseum (Maritime Museum).

St Antoniesbreestraat

Stretching south from Nieuwmarkt, St Antoniesbreestraat once linked the city centre with the Jewish quarter, but its huddle of shops and houses was mostly demolished in the 1980s to make way for a main road. The plan was subsequently abandoned, but the modern buildings that now line most of the street hardly fire the soul, even if the modern symmetries – and cubist, coloured panels – of the apartment blocks that spill along part of the street are visually arresting.

The Pintohuis

St Antoniesbreestraat 69. Mon & Wed 2–8pm, Fri 2–5pm, Sat 11am–4pm. Free. One of the few survivors of the development is the Pintohuis, which is now a public library. Easily spotted by its off-white Italianate facade, the mansion is named after Isaac de Pinto, a Jew who fled Portugal to escape the

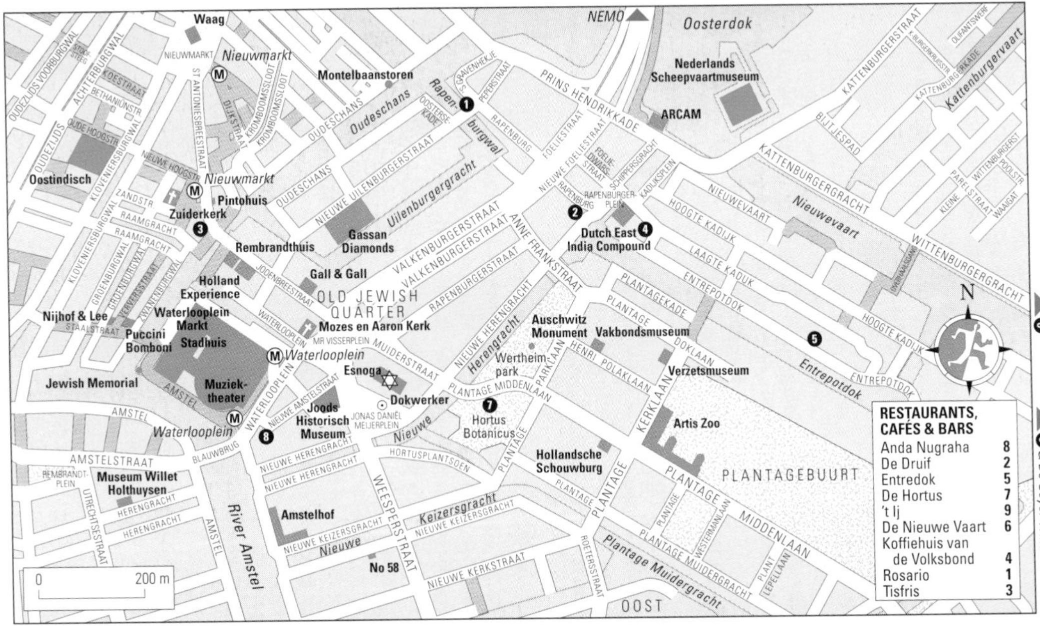
Waag
Nieuwmarkt
NIEUWMARKT
Montelbaanstoren
Rapen-
burgwal
Oudeschans
OUDESCHANS
NEMO
Oosterdok
Nederlands
Scheepvaartmuseum
ARCAM
PRINS HENDRIKKADE
KATTENBURGERSTRAAT
Kattenburgervaart
BIJTJESPAD
KATTENBURGERGRACHT
Nieuwevaart
NIEUWEVAART
WITTENBURGERGRACHT
PARELSTRAAT
KLEINE
WAAIGAT
POOLSTR
WITTENBURGERST
OLIFANTSWERF
OUDEZIJDS VOORBURGWAL
ACHTERBURGWAL
KOESTRAAT
BETHANIËNSTR
OUDE HOOGSTR
OUDEZIJDS
Oostindisch
KLOVENIERSBURGWAL
NIEUWE HOOGSTR
ST ANTONIESBREESTRAAT
DIJKSTRAAT
KROMBOOMSSLOOT
Pintohuis
Zuiderkerk
ZANDSTR
RAAMGRACHT
Rembrandthuis
Gassan
Diamonds
Uilenburgergracht
NIEUWE UILENBURGERSTRAAT
VALKENBURGERSTRAAT
RAPENBURGERSTRAAT
ANNE FRANKSTRAAT
RAPENBURG
PEPERSTRAAT
'S GRAVENHEKJE
OOSTERSE-KADE
FOELIESTRAAT
NIEUWE FOELIESTRAAT
FOELIE-DWARS-STRAAT
SCHIPPERSGRACHT
RAPENBURGER-PLEIN
KADIJKSPLEIN
Dutch East
India Compound
HOOGTE KADIJK
LAAGTE KADIJK
ENTREPOTDOK
Entrepotdok
PLANTAGEKADE
PLANTAGE
Gall & Gall
JODENBREESTRAAT
OLD JEWISH
QUARTER
Holland
Experience
Waterlooplein
Markt
Stadhuis
Nijhof & Lee
STAALSTRAAT
Puccini
Bomboni
GROENBURGWAL
ZWANENBURGWAL
Mozes en Aaron Kerk
MR VISSERPLEIN
MUIDERSTRAAT
Waterlooplein
Esnoga
Dokwerker
JONAS DANIËL
MEIJERPLEIN
Jewish Memorial
Muziek-
theater
AMSTEL
Joods
Historisch
Museum
NIEUWE AMSTELSTRAAT
NIEUWE HERENGRACHT
Herengracht
Auschwitz
Monument
Vakbondsmuseum
Wertheim-
park
PARKLAAN
HENRI POLAKLAAN
DOKLAAN
Verzetsmuseum
PLANTAGE MIDDENLAAN
Hortus
Botanicus
HORTUSPLANTSOEN
Nieuwe
Kerklaan
KERKLAAN
Artis Zoo
Hollandsche
Schouwburg
PLANTAGEBUURT
PLANTAGE
MIDDENLAAN
WESTERMANLAAN
PLANTAGE MUIDERGRACHT
Plantage Muidergracht
PLANT
LEPELLAAN
OOST
ROETERSSTRAAT
AMSTELSTRAAT
BLAUWBRUG
REMBRANDT-
PLEIN
Museum Willet
Holthuysen
UTRECHTSESTRAAT
HERENGRACHT
River Amstel
Amstelhof
NIEUWE KEIZERSGRACHT
Keizersgracht
WEESPERSTRAAT
No 58
NIEUWE KERKSTRAAT
0
200 m
N
6
9 & De Goyer Windmill
RESTAURANTS,
CAFÉS & BARS
Anda Nugraha 8
De Druif 2
Entredok 5
De Hortus 7
't Ij 9
De Nieuwe Vaart 6
Koffiehuis van
de Volksbond 4
Rosario 1
Tisfris 3

Inquisition and subsequently became a founder of the East India Company. Pinto bought the property in 1651 and promptly had it remodelled in grand style, the facade interrupted by six lofty pilasters, which lead the eye up to the blind balustrade. The mansion was the talk of the town, even more so when Pinto had the interior painted in a similar style to the front – pop in to look at the birds and cherubs of the original painted ceiling.

The Zuiderkerk

Mon 11am–4pm, Tues, Wed & Fri 9am–4pm, Thurs 9am–8pm. Free. The Zuiderkerk dates from 1611 and was designed by the prolific architect and sculptor Hendrick de Keyser, whose distinctive – and very popular – style extrapolated elements of traditional Flemish design, with fanciful detail and frilly towers added wherever possible. The basic design of the Zuiderkerk is firmly Gothic, but the soaring tower is typical of his work, complete with balconies and balustrades, arches and columns. Now deconsecrated, the church has itself been turned into a municipal information centre with displays on housing and the environment, plus temporary exhibitions revealing the city council's future plans. The tower, which has a separate entrance, can be climbed during the summer (June–Sept Wed–Sat 2–4pm; €3).

The Rembrandthuis

Jodenbreestraat 6. Mon–Sat 10am–5pm, Sun 1–5pm. €7. St Antoniesbreestraat runs into Jodenbreestraat, the "Broad Street of the Jews", at one time the main centre of Jewish activity. This ancient thoroughfare is short on charm, but it is home to the Rembrandthuis, whose intricate facade is decorated by pretty wooden shutters and a dinky pediment. Rembrandt bought this house at the height of his fame and popularity, living here for over twenty years and spending a fortune on furnishings – an expense that ultimately contributed to his bankruptcy. An inventory made at the time details the huge collection of paintings, sculptures and art treasures he'd amassed, almost all of which was auctioned off after he was declared insolvent and forced to move to a more modest house in the Jordaan in 1658.

The city council bought the Jodenbreestraat house in 1907 and has revamped the premises on several occasions, most recently in 1999. A visit begins in the modern building next door, but you're soon into the string of period rooms that have been returned to something like their appearance when

▼ REMBRANDTHUIS

Rembrandt lived here, with the inventory as a guide. The period furniture is enjoyable enough, especially the two box-beds, and the great man's studio is surprisingly large and well-lit, but the paintings that adorn the walls are almost entirely mediocre and there are no Rembrandts at all. More positively, two rooms beyond the period rooms hold an extensive collection of Rembrandt's etchings as well as several of the original copper plates on which he worked, and beyond them two further rooms are used for well-judged temporary displays of prints, usually – but not exclusively – by Dutch artists. To see Rembrandt's paintings you'll have to go to the Rijksmuseum (see p.128).

The Holland Experience

Jodenbreestraat 4 Ⓦ www.holland-experience.nl. Daily 10am–6pm. €8.50. The multimedia Holland Experience is a kind of sensory-bombardment movie about Holland and Amsterdam, with synchronized smells and a moving floor – not to mention the special 3D glasses. The experience lasts thirty minutes and is especially popular with school kids.

Gassan Diamonds

Nieuwe Uilenburgerstraat 173 Ⓣ 020/622 5333, Ⓦ www.gassandiamonds.com. Frequent 1hr guided tours daily 9am–5pm. Free. Gassan Diamonds occupies a large and imposing brick building dating from 1897. Before World War II, many local Jews worked as diamond cutters and polishers, though there's little sign of the industry here today, this factory being the main exception. Tours include a visit to the cutting and polishing areas as well a gambol round Gassan's diamond jewellery showroom; there's also a Delftware shop immediately outside the factory's main doors.

▼ WATERLOOPLEIN

The Stadhuis en Muziektheater

Ⓣ 020/625 5455, Ⓦ www.muziektheater.nl. Jodenbreestraat runs parallel to the Stadhuis en Muziektheater, a sprawling and rather undistinguished complex incorporating the city hall and an auditorium that was completed in 1986. The theatre's resident company, Netherlands Opera, offers the fullest, and most reasonably priced, programme of opera in Amsterdam. Tickets go very quickly, especially for the free lunchtime concerts held from September to May. One of the city's abiding ironies is that the title of the protest campaign aiming to prevent the development – "Stopera" – has passed into common usage to describe the finished item. Inside, amidst all the architectural mediocrity, there are a couple of minor attractions, beginning with the glass columns in the public passageway towards the rear of the complex. These give a salutary lesson on the fragility of the Netherlands: two contain water indicating the sea levels in the Dutch towns of Vlissingen and IJmuiden (below knee level), while another records the levels experienced during the 1953 flood disaster (way above head height). Downstairs a concrete pile shows what is known as "Normal Amsterdam Level" (NAP), originally calculated in 1684 as the average water level in the river IJ and still the basis for measuring altitude above sea level across Europe.

Waterlooplein

The indeterminate modernity of the Stadhuis complex dominates Waterlooplein, a rectangular parcel of land that was originally swampy marsh. This was the site of the first Jewish Quarter, but by the late nineteenth century it had become an insanitary slum. The slums were cleared in the 1880s and thereafter the open spaces of the Waterlooplein hosted the largest and liveliest market in the city, the place where Jews and Gentiles met to trade. In the war, the Germans used the square to round up their victims, but despite these ugly connotations the Waterlooplein was revived in the 1950s as the site of the city's main **flea market** (Mon–Sat 9am–5pm) and remains so to this day. It's nowhere near as large as it once was, but nonetheless it's still the final resting place of many a pair of yellow corduroy flares and has some wonderful antique/junk stalls to root through – second-hand vinyl too.

Mr Visserplein

Just behind the Muziektheater, on the corner of Mr Visserplein, is the Mozes en Aaron Kerk, a rather glum Neoclassical structure built on the site of a clandestine Catholic church in the 1840s. It takes its unusual name from a pair of facade stones bearing effigies of the two prophets that decorated an earlier building which it replaced. Earlier still, the site was occupied by the house where the philosopher and theologian Spinoza was born in 1632. The square itself, a busy junction for traffic speeding towards the IJ tunnel, takes its name from Mr Visser, President of the Supreme Court of the Netherlands in 1939. He was dismissed the following year when the Germans occupied the country, and became an active member of the Jewish resistance, working for the illegal underground newspaper *Het Parool* ("The Password") and refusing to wear the yellow Star of David. He died in 1942, a few days after publicly – and famously – denouncing all forms of collaboration.

▼ MOZES EN AARON KERK

▲ THE ESNOGA

The Esnoga

Mr Visserplein. Sun–Fri 10am–4pm; closed Yom Kippur. €5. The brown and bulky brickwork of the Esnoga or Portuguese synagogue was completed in 1675 for the city's Sephardic community. One of Amsterdam's most imposing buildings, it has been barely altered since its construction, its lofty interior following the Sephardic tradition in having the *Hechal* (the Ark of the Covenant) and *tebah* (from where services are led) at opposite ends. Also traditional is the seating, with two sets of wooden benches (for the men) facing each other across the central aisle – the women have separate galleries up above. A set of superb brass chandeliers holds the candles that remain the only source of artificial light. When it was completed, the synagogue was one of the largest in the world, its congregation almost certainly the richest; today, the Sephardic community has dwindled to just a few dozen members, most of whom live outside the city centre. In one of the outhouses, a video sheds light on the history of the synagogue and Amsterdam's Sephardim; the mystery is why the Germans left it alone – no one knows for sure, but it seems likely that they intended to turn it into a museum once all the Jews had been polished off.

Jonas Daniel Meijerplein

Jonas Daniel Meijerplein was where in February 1941 around 400 Jewish men were forcibly loaded up on trucks and taken to their deaths at Mauthausen concentration camp, in reprisal for the killing of a Dutch Nazi during a street fight. The arrests sparked off the February Strike, a general strike in protest against the Germans' treatment of the Jews. It was organized by the outlawed Communist Party and spearheaded by Amsterdam's transport workers and dockers – a rare demonstration of solidarity with the Jews whose fate was usually accepted without visible protest in all of occupied Europe. The strike was quickly suppressed, but is still commemorated by an annual wreath-laying ceremony on February 25, as well as by Mari Andriessen's statue of the Dokwerker (Dockworker) here on the square.

Joods Historisch Museum

J.D. Meijerplein ⓦ www.jhm.nl. Daily 11am–5pm, closed Yom Kippur. €6.50. The Joods Historisch Museum – the Jewish Historical Museum – is cleverly located in four Ashkenazi synagogues dating from the late seventeenth century. For years after the war these buildings lay abandoned, but they were finally refurbished – and connected by walkways – in the 1980s to accommodate a Jewish resource centre and exhibition area. The latter is located in the handsome Grote Synagoge of 1671 and features a fairly small but wide-ranging collection covering most aspects of Dutch Jewish life. Downstairs, in the main body of the synagogue, is a fine collection of religious silverware as well as a handful of paintings and all manner of antique artefacts illustrating religious customs and practices. The gallery above holds a social history of the city's Jews, tracing their prominent role in a wide variety of industries, and examining the trauma of World War II, complete with several especially moving photographs.

The Plantagebuurt

Developed in the middle of the nineteenth century, the Plantagebuurt, with its comfortable streets spreading to either side of Plantage Middenlaan boulevard, was built as part of a concerted attempt to provide good-quality housing for the city's expanding middle classes. Although it was never as fashionable as the older residential parts of the Grachtengordel, the new district did contain elegant villas and spacious terraces, making it a first suburban port of call for many aspiring Jews. Nowadays, the Plantagebuurt is still one of the more prosperous parts of the city, in a modest sort of way, and boasts two especially enjoyable attractions – the Hortus Botanicus botanical gardens and the Verzetsmuseum (Dutch Resistance Museum).

▼ DE DOKWERKER

Hortus Botanicus

Plantage Middenlaan 2a. Mon–Fri 9am–5pm, Sat & Sun 10am–5pm; closes 4pm in Dec & Jan. €6. Amsterdam's Hortus Botanicus botanical gardens were founded in 1682 as medicinal gardens for the use of the city's physicians and apothecaries. Thereafter, many of the city's merchants made a point of bringing back exotic species from the East, the result being the 6000-odd plant species exhibited today. The gardens are divided into several distinct sections. Outside are twenty four distinctive types of tree, each clearly labelled and its location pinpointed by a map available at the entrance kiosk. There's also a three-climates glasshouse, where the plants are arranged according to their geographical origins, a palm house, a Californian desert hothouse, an orchid nursery and a butterfly house. It's all very low-key – and none the worse for that – and the gardens make a relaxing break on any tour of central Amsterdam, especially as the café, in the old orangery, serves up tasty sandwiches, coffee and cakes from 11am to 3pm.

Wertheimpark

The pocket-sized Wertheimpark, across the road from the Hortus Botanicus, is home to the Auschwitz monument, a simple affair with symbolically broken mirrors and an inscription that reads *Nooit meer Auschwitz* ("Auschwitz – Never Again"). It was designed by the Dutch writer Jan Wolkers.

De Hollandsche Schouwburg

Plantage Middenlaan 24. Daily 11am–4pm except Yom Kippur. Free. Another sad relic of the war, De Hollandsche Schouwburg was once a thriving Jewish theatre, but the Germans turned it into the main assembly point for Amsterdam Jews prior to their deportation. Inside, there was no daylight and families were interned in conditions that foreshadowed those of the camps they would soon be taken to. The building has been refurbished to house a small exhibition on the plight of the city's Jews, but the old auditorium out at the back has been left as an empty, roofless shell. A memorial column of basalt on a Star of David base stands where the stage once was, an intensely mournful monument to suffering of unfathomable proportions.

Artis Zoo

Plantage Kerklaan 38–40 ⓣ020/523 3400, ⓦwww.artis.nl. Daily: April to mid-Oct 9am–6pm; mid-Oct to March 9am–5pm. €14.50, 3- to 9-year-olds €11. Opened in 1838, Artis Zoo is the oldest zoo in the country, and is now one of the city's top tourist attractions, though thankfully its layout and refreshing lack of bars and cages mean that it never feels overcrowded. Highlights include an African savanna environment, a seventy-metre-long aviary, aquaria and a South American zone with llamas and the world's largest rodent, the capibara. In addition, the on-site Planetarium has five or six shows daily, all in Dutch, though you can pick up a leaflet with an English translation from the desk. Feeding times – always popular – are as follows: 11am birds of prey; 11.30am and 3.45pm seals and sea lions; 2pm pelicans; 2.30pm crocodiles (Sun only); 3pm lions and tigers (not Fri); 3.30pm penguins.

Vakbondsmuseum

Henri Polaklaan 9. Tues–Fri 11am–5pm, Sun 1–5pm. €4. The Vakbondsmuseum (Trade Union Museum) contains a small exhibition of documents, cuttings and photos relating to the Dutch labour movement, with a section devoted to Henri Polak, the leader of the Diamond Workers' Union and the man responsible for coordinating the successful campaign for the eight-hour working day. However, the building is actually rather more interesting than the exhibition. Built by Berlage for the Diamond Workers' Union in 1900, it was designed in a distinctive style that incorporated Romanesque features within an Expressionist framework. The striking, brightly coloured interior develops these themes with a beautiful mixture of stained-glass windows, stone arches, painted brickwork and patterned tiles. From the outside, the building looks like a fortified mansion, hence its old nickname the Rode Burgt ("Red Stronghold"). This design was not just about Berlage's whims. Acting on behalf of the employers, the police – and sometimes armed scabs – were regularly used to break strikes, and the union believed that members could hold out here in relative safety, which they did on more than one occasion.

▲ ENTREPOTDOK

Verzetsmuseum

Plantage Kerklaan 61
ⓦ www.verzetsmuseum.org. Tues–Fri 10am–5pm, Mon, Sat & Sun noon–5pm. €5.

The excellent Verzetsmuseum (Dutch Resistance Museum) outlines the development of the Dutch Resistance from the German invasion of the Netherlands in May 1940 to the country's liberation in 1945. Thoughtfully presented, the main gangway examines the experience of the majority of the population, dealing honestly with the fine balance between cooperation and collaboration. Side rooms are devoted to different aspects of the resistance, from the brave determination of the Communist Party, who went underground as soon as the Germans arrived, to more ad hoc responses like the so-called Milk Strike of 1943, when hundreds of milk producers refused to deliver.

Fascinating old photographs illustrate the (English and Dutch) text along with a host of original artefacts, from examples of illegal newsletters to signed German death warrants. Apart from their treatment of the Jews, which is detailed here, perhaps the most chilling feature of the occupation was the use of indiscriminate reprisals to terrify the population. The museum has dozens of little metal sheets providing biographical sketches of the members of the Resistance – and it's this mixture of the general and the personal that is its real strength.

The Oosterdok

Just to the north of the Plantagebuurt lies the Oosterdok, whose network of artificial islands was dredged out of the River IJ to increase Amsterdam's shipping facilities in the seventeenth century. By the 1980s, this mosaic of docks, jetties and islands had become something of a post-industrial eyesore, but since then an ambitious redevelopment programme has turned things around and the area is now dotted with worthwhile attractions, principally the Nederlands Scheepvaartmuseum. Easily the most agreeable way of reaching the Oosterdok is via the footbridge at the north end of Plantage Kerklaan – metres from the Verzetsmuseum (see p.123) – which leads to the Entrepotdok.

Entrepotdok

Over the footbridge at the end of Plantage Kerklaan lies the most interesting of the Oosterdok islands, a slender rectangle whose southern quayside, Entrepotdok, is lined by a long series of nineteenth-century gabled warehouses that were once part of the largest warehouse complex in continental Europe, a gigantic customs-free zone established for goods in transit. On the ground floor, above the main entrance, each warehouse sports the name of a town or island; goods for onward transportation were stored in the appropriate warehouse until there were enough to fill a boat or barge. The warehouses have been tastefully converted into offices and apartments, a fate that must surely befall the central East India Company compound, whose chunky Neoclassical entrance is at the west end of Entrepotdok on Kadijksplein.

The Nederlands Scheepvaartmuseum

Kattenburgerplein
www.scheepvaartmuseum.nl.
Tues–Sun 10am–5pm; mid-June to mid-Sept also Mon 10am–5pm. €7.50.

From Kadijksplein, it's the briefest of strolls over to the conspicuous Nederlands Scheepvaartmuseum (Netherlands Maritime Museum), which occupies the old arsenal of the Dutch navy, a vast sandstone structure that is underpinned by no less than 18,000 wooden piles driven deep into the river bed at enormous expense in the 1650s.

It's the perfect location for a maritime museum, though to the non-specialist the sheer number of ship models can be a tad repetitive. The collection is spread over three floors, begin-

▼ SCHEEPVAARTMUSEUM

ning on the ground floor which is used to host temporary exhibitions as well as a flashy gilded barge built for King William I of the Netherlands in 1818. The next floor up, largely devoted to shipping in the seventeenth and eighteenth centuries, is the best, and includes garish ships' figureheads and tillers, examples of early atlases and navigational equipment, and finely detailed models of the clippers of the East India Company, then the fastest ships in the world. There are a number of nautical paintings too, the best by Willem van de Velde II (or The Younger; 1633–1707), who was the most successful of the Dutch marine painters of the period. His canvases emphasize the strength and power of the Dutch warship, often depicted in battle or amidst turbulent seas. The final floor is devoted to the nineteenth and early twentieth centuries. Once again there are models galore, but the paintings are perhaps more enjoyable, melodramatic canvases of stormy seas and brave sailing ships. Outside, moored at the museum jetty, is the most popular exhibit by a long chalk, a full-scale replica of an East Indiaman, the *Amsterdam*, that is crewed by enthusiastic nautical actors.

ARCAM

Prins Hendrikkade 600 ⓣ020/620 4878, ⓦwww.arcam.nl. Tues–Sat 1–5pm. Free. Strolling west from the Maritime Museum along the waterfront, you'll soon spy the idiosyncratic hood-shaped structure that has been built to house the Amsterdam Centre for Architecture, otherwise ARCAM. There are architectural displays here, sometimes of a theoretical nature and sometimes forewarning the city of what its architects have in mind, as well as public lectures and discussions.

▲ DE GOOYER WINDMILL

NEMO

Prins Hendrikkade ⓣ0900/9191100, ⓦwww.e-nemo.nl. Tues–Sun 10am–5pm, plus Mon 10am–5pm during school holidays, July & Aug. €11. Back outside the ARCAM building, the foreground is dominated by a massive elevated hood that rears up above the entrance to the IJ tunnel. A good part of this is occupied by the large and lavish NEMO centre, a (pre-teenage) kids' attraction par excellence, with all sorts of interactive science and technological exhibits spread over six floors and set out under four broad themes: Physics, Technology, Information Technology and Bio-science behaviour.

The De Gooyer Windmill

Funenkade 5.

East of the Maritime Museum along Hoogte Kadijk is the De Gooyer Windmill, standing tall beside a long and slender canal. Amsterdam was once dotted with windmills, used for pumping water and grinding corn, and this is one of the few surviving grain mills; its sails still turn on the first Saturday of the month – wind permitting. Also a brewery (see opposite).

Shops

Gall & Gall

Jodenbreestraat 23 ⓣ020/428 7060. Outstanding range of Dutch jenevers (gins) and flavoured spirits. Also has a good stock of imported wines. Part of a popular chain.

Nijhof & Lee

Staalstraat 13a ⓣ020/620 3980, ⓦwww.nijhoflee.nl. Closed Sun. One of the city's best art bookshops with a raft of English-language titles. Good for photography too. Mostly new books, but some rare and antique ones as well.

Puccini Bomboni

Staalstraat 17 ⓣ020/626 5474. Excellent chocolatier with a fine range of handmade chocolates and attentive service. None of the tweeness of some of its competitors – the decor is briskly modern.

Restaurants

Anda Nugraha

Waterlooplein 369 ⓣ020/626 6064. Lively restaurant serving inexpensive Indonesian food. Well-prepared, moderately spicy dishes using the freshest of ingredients, but the selection is small. There's a very pleasant terrace in the summer.

Koffiehuis van de Volksbond

Kadijksplein 4 ⓣ020/622 1209. Formerly a Communist Party café and apparently the place where the local dockworkers used to receive their wages, this is now an Oosterdok neighbourhood café-restaurant.

Rosario

Peperstraat 10 ⓣ020/627 0280. Closed Sun & Mon. Very attractive restaurant slightly out of the way in a relatively unexplored corner of Amsterdam. Good Italian food.

Bars and cafés

De Druif

Rapenburgerplein 83. Possibly the city's oldest bar, and certainly one of its more beguiling, yet hardly anyone knows about it. Its popularity with the locals lends it a village pub feel.

Entredok

Entrepotdok 64. Perhaps the best of a growing number of bars in this newly renovated area. The clientele hails from the sur-

▼ ENTREDOK

rounding hi-tech offices, though increasingly from the residential blocks in between, too.

De Groene Olifant

Sarphatistraat 126. Metres from the Muiderpoort, this is a characterful old wood-panelled brown café, with floor-to-ceiling windows and an excellent, varied menu.

De Hortus

Plantage Middenlaan 2a. Daily 11am–3pm. Amenable café in the orangery of the botanical gardens – the Hortus Botanicus. Good range of tasty sandwiches and rolls plus the best blueberry cheesecake in the Western world. Inexpensive.

't Ij

De Gooyer Windmill, Funenkade 7. Wed–Sun 3–8pm. The beers (Natte, Zatte and Struis), brewed on the premises, are extremely strong. A good place to drink yourself silly.

De Nieuwe Vaart

Oostenburgergracht 187. Traditional Dutch café with slots for amateur singers.

Tisfris

St Antoniesbreestraat 142. Colourful, New Age-ish split-level café-cum-bar near the Rembrandt House. Youthful and popular.

Clubs and venues

De Ijsbreker

Weesperzijde 23 ⓣ020/693 9093, ⓦwww.ijsbreker.nl. Out of the town centre by the Amstel, with a delightful terrace on the water. Has a large, varied programme of international modern, chamber and experimental music, as well as featuring obscure, avant-garde local performers. Concerts are occasionally held in the Planetarium of the Artis Zoo.

▼ 'T IJ

The Museum Quarter and the Vondelpark

During the nineteenth century, Amsterdam burst out of its restraining canals, gobbling up the surrounding countryside. These new outlying suburbs were mostly residential, but Amsterdam's leading museums were packed into a relatively small area around the edge of Museumplein. The largest of the museums was – and remains – the Rijksmuseum, which occupies a huge late nineteenth-century edifice overlooking the Singelgracht. Possessing an exceptional collection of Dutch paintings from the fifteenth to the seventeenth century, it is perhaps best known for its series of paintings by Rembrandt. Close by, the much newer Van Gogh Museum boasts the finest assortment of Van Gogh paintings in the world, but the adjacent Stedelijk Museum, which has long occupied a grand neo-Renaissance building dating from 1895, is closed for refurbishment until 2008; in the meantime some of its outstanding permanent collection of modern art is on display in the old postal building near Centraal Station (see p.75).

Museumplein

Extending south from Stadhouderskade to Van Baerlestraat, Museumplein is Amsterdam's largest open space, its wide lawns and gravelled spaces used for a variety of outdoor activities, from visiting circuses to political demonstrations. There's a war memorial here too – it's the group of slim steel blocks about three-quarters of the way down the Museumplein on the left-hand side and it commemorates the women of of the wartime concentration camps, particularly the thousands who died at Ravensbruck. The text reads: "For those women who defied fascism until the bitter end".

The Rijksmuseum

Entrance to the Philips Wing is on Jan Luijkenstraat ⓦwww.rijksmuseum.nl. Daily 9am–6pm. €9.

The Rijksmuseum is without question the country's foremost museum, with one of the world's most comprehensive collections of seventeenth-century Dutch paintings, including twenty or so of Rembrandt's works, plus a healthy sample of canvases by Steen, Hals, Vermeer and their leading contemporaries. The museum also owns an extravagant collection of paintings from every other pre-twentieth-century period of Dutch art and has a vast hoard of applied art and sculpture. The bad news is that there's a major **renovation** going on at the moment and most of

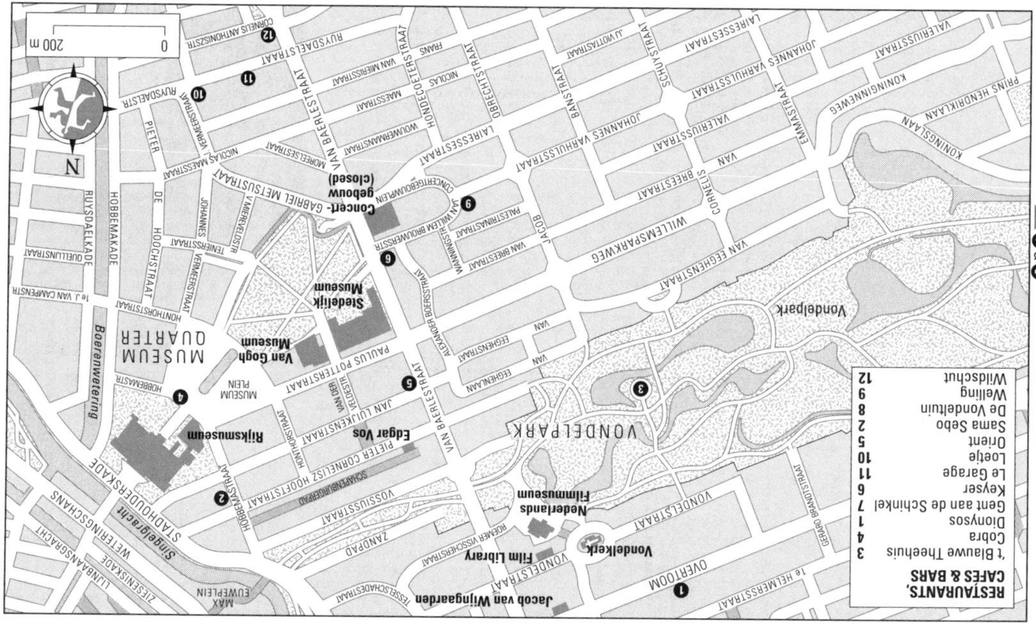
RESTAURANTS, CAFÉS & BARS
't Blauwe Theehuis 3
Cobra 4
Dionysos 1
Gent aan de Schinkel 7
Keyser 6
Le Garage 11
Loetje 10
Orient 5
Sama Sebo 2
De Vondeltuin 8
Welling 9
Wildschut 12
MUSEUM QUARTER
VONDELPARK
Rijksmuseum
Van Gogh Museum
Stedelijk Museum
Concert- gebouw (closed)
Nederlands Filmmuseum
Film Library
Vondelkerk
Edgar Vos
Jacob van Wijngaarden
Vondelpark
MUSEUM PLEIN
N
0
200 m
7 & 8

▲ *WOMAN READING A LETTER*, JAN VERMEER, RIJKSMUSEUM

the museum is closed. The exception is the Rijksmuseum's **Philips Wing**, whose smallish but eclectic "Masterpieces" exhibition, scheduled to last until the rest of the museum is reopened, is devoted to the paintings of Amsterdam's Golden Age. On display are, for example, several wonderful canvases by Frans Hals, the soft, tonal river scenes of the Haarlem artist Salomon van Ruysdael and the cool church interiors of Pieter Saenredam. There are also portraits by Ferdinand, the carousing peasants of Jan Steen, and the cool interiors of Vermeer, Gerard ter Borch and Pieter de Hooch. However, it's the Rembrandts that steal the show, especially *The Night Watch* of 1642 – perhaps the most famous and probably the most valuable of all the artist's pictures – plus other key works, like a late *Self-Portrait*, a touching depiction of his cowled son, *Titus*, and *The Jewish Bride*, one of his very last pictures, finished in 1667.

The Van Gogh Museum

ⓦ www.vangoghmuseum.nl. Daily 10am–6pm. €9, children 13–17 years €2.50. The **Van Gogh Museum**, comprising a fabulous collection of the artist's (1853–1890) work, is one of Amsterdam's top attractions. The museum occupies two modern buildings, with the kernel of the collection housed in an angular building designed by a leading light of the De Stijl movement, Gerritt Rietveld, and opened to the public in 1973. Well-conceived and beautifully presented, this part of the museum provides an introduction to the man and his art based on paintings that were mostly inherited from Vincent's art-dealer brother Theo. To the rear of Rietveld's building, and connected by a ground-floor-level escalator, is the ultra-modern annexe, an aesthetically controversial structure completed in 1998. The annexe was financed by a Japanese insurance company – the same conglomerate who paid $35 million for one of Van Gogh's *Sunflowers* canvases in 1987 – and provides temporary exhibition space. Most of these exhibitions focus on one aspect or another of Van Gogh's art and draw heavily on the permanent collection, which means that the paintings displayed in the older building are regularly rotated.

The **ground floor** of the main museum displays works by some of Van Gogh's well-known friends and contemporaries, many of whom influenced his work – Gauguin, Millet, Anton Mauve, Charles Daubigny and others – while the **first floor** has paintings by the artist himself, displayed chronologically, starting with the dark, sombre works of the early years like *The Potato Eaters* and finishing up with the asylum years at St Rémy and the final, tortured paintings done at Auvers, where Van Gogh lodged for the last three months of his life. It was at Auvers that he painted the frantic *Ears of Wheat* and *Wheatfield with a Reaper*, in which the fields swirl and writhe under weird, light-green, moving skies. It was a few weeks after completing these last paintings that Van Gogh shot and fatally wounded himself.

The two floors above provide a back-up to the main collection. The **second floor** has a study area with PC access to a detailed computerized account of Van Gogh's life and times, plus a number of sketches and a handful of less familiar paintings. The **third floor** features more drawings and sketches from the permanent collection as well as notebooks and letters. This floor also affords space to relevant temporary exhibitions illustrating Van Gogh's artistic influences, or his own influence on other artists.

The Concertgebouw

Concertgebouwplein 2–6 ⓣ020/671 8345, ⓦwww.concertgebouw.nl.

The **Concertgebouw** (Concert Hall) is the home of the famed – and much recorded – Koninklijk (Royal) Concertgebouw Orchestra. When the German composer Brahms visited

Rembrandt

Born in Leiden to a family of millers, **Rembrandt Harmenszoon van Rijn** (1606–1669) picked up his first important artistic tips as an apprentice to Pieter Lastman in Amsterdam in the early 1620s. It was here that Rembrandt developed a penchant for mythological and religious subjects, vividly light and rendered with a smooth and glossy finish. After his apprenticeship, in around 1625, Rembrandt returned to Leiden to establish himself as an independent master painter and, this achieved, he returned to Amsterdam some six years later, where he stayed for the rest of his life. In the early 1630s, Rembrandt concentrated on **portrait painting**, churning out dozens of pictures of the burghers of his day, a profitable business that made him both well-to-do and well known. In 1634 he married **Saskia van Uylenburch** and five years later the couple moved into a smart house on Jodenbreestraat, now the Rembrandthuis museum (see p.117). Things seemed set fair, and certainly Rembrandt's portraits of his wife are tender and loving, but these years were marred by the death of all but one of his children in infancy, the sole survivor being the much-loved **Titus** (1641–1668).

In 1642, Rembrandt produced what has become his most celebrated painting, *The Night Watch*, but thereafter his career went into decline, essentially because he forsook portraiture to focus on increasingly sombre and introspective **religious works**. Traditionally, Rembrandt's change of artistic direction has been tied in with the death of Saskia in 1642, but although it is certainly true that Rembrandt was grief-stricken, he was also facing increased competition from a new batch of portrait artists, primarily Ferdinand Bol and Govert Flinck. Whatever the reason, there were few customers for Rembrandt's religious works and he made matters worse by refusing to adjust his spending. The crunch came in 1656, when he was formally declared insolvent, and four years later he was obliged to sell his house and goods, moving to much humbler premises in the Jordaan (see p.107). By this time, he had a new cohabitee, **Hendrickje Stoffels** (a clause in Saskia's will prevented them from ever marrying), and, in the early 1660s, she and Titus took Rembrandt in hand, sorting out his finances and making him their employee. With his money problems solved, a relieved Rembrandt then produced some of his finest paintings, emotionally deep and contemplative works with a rough finish, the paint often daubed almost trowel-like. Hendrickje died in 1663, Titus in 1668, a year before his father.

▲ VONDELKERK

Amsterdam in the 1870s he was scathing about the locals' lack of culture and in particular their lack of an even halfway suitable venue for his music. In the face of such ridicule, a consortium of Amsterdam businessmen got together to fund the construction of a brand-new concert hall and the result was the Concertgebouw, completed in 1888. Since then it has become renowned among musicians and concertgoers for its marvellous acoustics, and after a facelift and the replacement of its crumbling foundations in the early 1990s it is looking – and sounding – better than ever. The acoustics of the Grote Zaal (Large Hall) are unparalleled, and the smaller Kleine Zaal regularly hosts chamber concerts, often by the resident Borodin Quartet. Prices are very reasonable, €30–50, there are free Wednesday lunchtime concerts from September to May, and in July and August they put on a heavily subsidized series of summer concerts.

The Vondelpark

Amsterdam is short of green spaces, which makes the leafy expanses of the Vondelpark, a short stretch from Museumplein (and the Concertgebouw), doubly welcome. This is easily the largest and most popular of the city's parks, its network of footpaths used by a healthy slice of the city's population. The park dates back to 1864, when a group of leading Amsterdammers clubbed together to transform the soggy marshland that lay beyond the Leidsepoort into a landscaped park. Named after the popular seventeenth-century poet Joost van den Vondel, the park possesses over 100 species of tree, a wide variety of local and imported plants, and – amongst many incidental features – a bandstand, an excellent rose garden, and a network of ponds and narrow waterways that are home to many sorts of wildfowl. There are other animals too: cows, sheep, hundreds of squirrels, plus, bizarrely enough, a large colony of bright-green parakeets. During the summer the park regularly hosts free concerts and theatrical performances, mostly in its own specially designed open-air theatre.

The Vondelkerk

The Vondelkerk, with its lugubrious brown brick hull and

whopping spire, has had more than its share of bad luck. Work on the church, which was designed by Cuypers – the architect of Centraal Station and the Rijksmuseum – began in 1872, but the finances ran out the following year and the building was not completed till the 1880s. Twenty years later it was struck by lightning and in the ensuing fire its tower was burnt to a cinder – the present one was added much later. The church always struggled to find a decent-sized congregation, but limped on until it was finally deconsecrated in 1979, being turned into offices thereafter.

The Nederlands Filmmuseum and Library

Vondelpark 3 ⓣ020/589 1400, ⓦwww.filmmuseum.nl. Housed in a glum, nineteenth-century building near the northeast corner of the Vondelpark, the Nederlands Filmmuseum is really more an arthouse cinema (with two screens) than a museum, a showcase for avant-garde films – most of which are shown in their original language, with subtitles in Dutch or sometimes English. There are several screenings nightly, plus regular matinees, and the programme often follows a prescribed theme or subject. Look out also for news of the free screenings of classic movies in the summer. Metres away, at Vondelstraat 69, the museum's **film library** (Tues–Thurs 10am–5pm, Sat 11am–5pm) has a substantial collection of books, magazines and journals, some in English, though they are for reference only.

▼ FILMMUSEUM

Shops

Jacob van Wijngaarden

Overtoom 97 ⓣ020/612 1901. The city's best travel bookshop, with knowledgeable staff and a huge selection of books and maps. Also inflatable and illuminated globes.

Edgar Vos

P.C. Hooftstraat 136 ⓣ020/671 2748. Flagship store of the Dutch *haute couture* designer – power dressing for women and a good casual range too.

Cafés and tearooms

CoBrA

Museumplein. A modern café set up during the renovation of the square, with paintings from the twentieth-century CoBrA movement. The terrace has become the new hotspot for Amsterdam's professional couples and their kids. The club sandwiches are pricey but good, but the coffee could be better.

▼ COBRA

Keyser

Van Baerlestraat 96 ☎020/671 1441. Closed Sun. In operation since 1905, and right next to the Concertgebouw, this café/restaurant exudes a *fin-de-siècle* charm, with ferns, gliding bow-tied waiters, and a dark carved-wood interior. Prices are slightly above average, especially for the food, but it's a wonderful place nonetheless. You'll need to make bookings for the restaurant, and dress accordingly.

Welling

J.W. Brouwersstraat 32. Supposedly the traditional haunt of the gloomy Amsterdam intellectual, this café-cum-bar is usually packed solid with performers and visitors from the Concertgebouw next door.

Restaurants

Dionysos

Overtoom 176 ☎020/689 4441. Daily 5pm–1am. Inexpensive Greek restaurant a little to the south of Leidseplein, with the distinct added advantage of serving until 1am. Phone ahead if you're going to turn up after midnight.

Gent aan de Schinkel

Theophile de Bockstraat 1 ☎020/388 2851. Lovely corner restaurant on a busy canal. Belgian and fusion cuisine and a huge range of bottled Belgian beers to enjoy on their summer terrace. Just outside the other entrance to the Vondelpark, across the cyclist bridge. Moderately priced.

Le Garage

Ruysdaelstraat 54 ☎020/679 7176. Daily 6–11pm, Mon–Fri also noon–2pm. This elegant and pricey restaurant is popular with a media crowd, since it's run by a well-known Dutch TV cook. An eclectic French and Italian menu; call to reserve a week ahead, dress to impress and bring at least €35 or so per person.

Loetje

Joh Vermeerstraat 52 ☎020/662 8173. One of the two best steakhouses in town (the other one being *Piet de Leeuw*, see p.98). Kitchen open 11am–10pm, closed on Sun, Sat no lunch. Moderate prices.

▲ KEYSER

Orient

Van Baerlestraat 21 ⓣ020/673 4958. Moderate to expensive Indonesian restaurant. Excellently prepared dishes, with a wide range to choose from; vegetarians are very well taken care of, and the service is generally good. Expect to pay around €25 for a *rijsttafel*.

Sama Sebo

P.C. Hooftstraat 27 ⓣ020/662 8146. Closed Sun. Amsterdam's best-known Indonesian restaurant, especially for its delicious *rijsttafel* (€25). If you are on a tight budget, the prices may initially put you off, but it's easy to eat quite reasonably by choosing à la carte dishes, and the food is usually great.

Bars

't Blauwe Theehuis

Vondelpark 5 ⓦwww.blauwetheehuis.nl. Daily 9am till late. Beautiful tea-room/café/bar housed in a circular building from the De Stijl period. A good place for breakfast and for open-air dancing with DJs on Fri & Sat nights; jazz on Thurs.

De Vondeltuin

Vondelpark 7 ⓣ020/664 5091. April–Oct daily 11am–1am; Nov–March Sat & Sun noon–5pm. Peaceful terrace on the Amstelveen side of the Vondelpark serving tapas, fresh salads and pancakes, next to the in-line skate rental. A picnic or barbecue in the park including skate rental can be arranged for around €20.

Wildschut

Roelof Hartplein 1. Large and congenial bar famous for its Art Deco trimmings. Not far from the Concertgebouw and with examples of the Amsterdam School of Architecture.

The outer districts

Amsterdam is a small city, and the majority of its residential outer districts are easily reached from the city centre. The south holds most of interest, kicking off with the raucous De Pijp quarter, home to the Heineken Experience, sited in the company's old brewery, and the 1930s architecture of the Nieuw Zuid (New South), which also contains the enjoyable woodland area of the Amsterdamse Bos. As for the other districts, you'll find a good deal less reason to make the effort, although the Tropenmuseum, a short walk from the Muiderpoort gate in Amsterdam East, is worth a special journey.

De Pijp

Across Boerenwetering, the canal to the east of the Rijksmuseum and Museumplein (see p.128), lies the busy heart of the Oud Zuid (Old South) – the district known as De Pijp ("The Pipe"), Amsterdam's first real suburb. New development beyond the Singelgracht began around 1870, but after laying down the street plans, the city council left the actual house-building to private developers. They made the most of the arrangement and constructed long rows of cheaply built and largely featureless five- and six-storey buildings and it is these which still dominate the area today. The district's name comes from the characteristically narrow terraced streets running between long, sombre canyons of brick tenements: the apartments here were said to resemble pipe-drawers, since each had a tiny street frontage but extended deep into the building. De Pijp remains one of the city's more closely knit communities, and is home to a large proportion of new immigrants – Surinamese, Moroccan, Turkish and Asian.

Trams #16 and #24, beginning at Centraal Station, travel along the northern part of De Pijp's main drag, Ferdinand Bolstraat, as far as Albert Cuypstraat.

▼ DE PIJP STREET SCENE

The Heineken Experience

Stadhouderskade 78 ⓣ020/523 9666 ⓦwww.heinekenexperience.com. Tues–Sun 10am–6pm. €10. On the northern edge of De Pijp, the former Heineken brewery, a whopping modern building beside the Singelgracht canal, now holds the Heineken

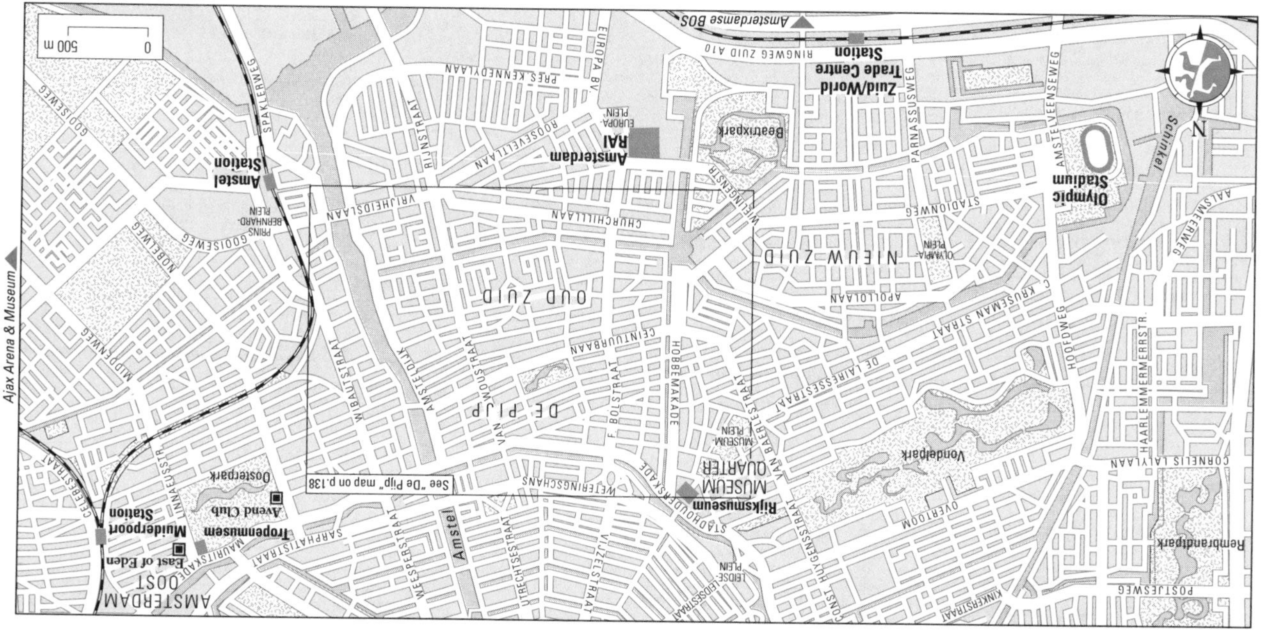
Ajax Arena & Museum
0
500 m
AMSTERDAM
OOST
East of Eden
Muiderpoort
Station
Tropenmusem
Avend Club
Oosterpark
CELEBESSTRAAT
LINNAEUSSTR.
MAURITSKADE
SARPHATISTRAAT
MIDDENWEG
NOBELWEG
GOOISEWEG
PRINS
BERNHARD-
PLEIN
Amstel
Station
SPAKLERWEG
See "De Pijp" map on p.138
WIBAUTSTRAAT
WEESPERSTRAAT
Amstel
AMSTELDIJK
VRIJHEIDSLAAN
RIJNSTRAAT
VAN
WOUSTRAAT
DE PIJP
OUD ZUID
UTRECHTSESTRAAT
VIJZELSTRAAT
WETERINGSCHANS
F. BOLSTRAAT
CEINTUURBAAN
CHURCHILLLAAN
ROOSEVELTLAAN
PRES. KENNEDYLAAN
Amsterdam
RAI
EUROPA-
PLEIN
EUROPA BV.
STADHOUDERSKADE
HOBBEMAKADE
LEIDSESTRAAT
LEIDSE-
PLEIN
Rijksmuseum
MUSEUM
QUARTER
MUSEUM-
PLEIN
VAN BAERLESTRAAT
WIELINGENSTR.
Beatrixpark
RINGWEG ZUID A10
Amsterdamse BOS
CONST. HUYGENSSTRAAT
DE LAIRESSESTRAAT
NIEUW ZUID
APOLLOLAAN
Zuid/World
Trade Centre
Station
OVERTOOM
Vondelpark
OLYMPIA-
PLEIN
STADIONWEG
PARNASSUSWEG
KINKERSTRAAT
C. KRUSEMAN STRAAT
HOOFDWEG
Olympic
Stadium
AMSTELVEENSEWEG
POSTJESWEG
CORNELIS LALYLAAN
HAARLEMMERMERRSTR.
Rembrandtpark
Schinkel
AALSMEERWEG
N

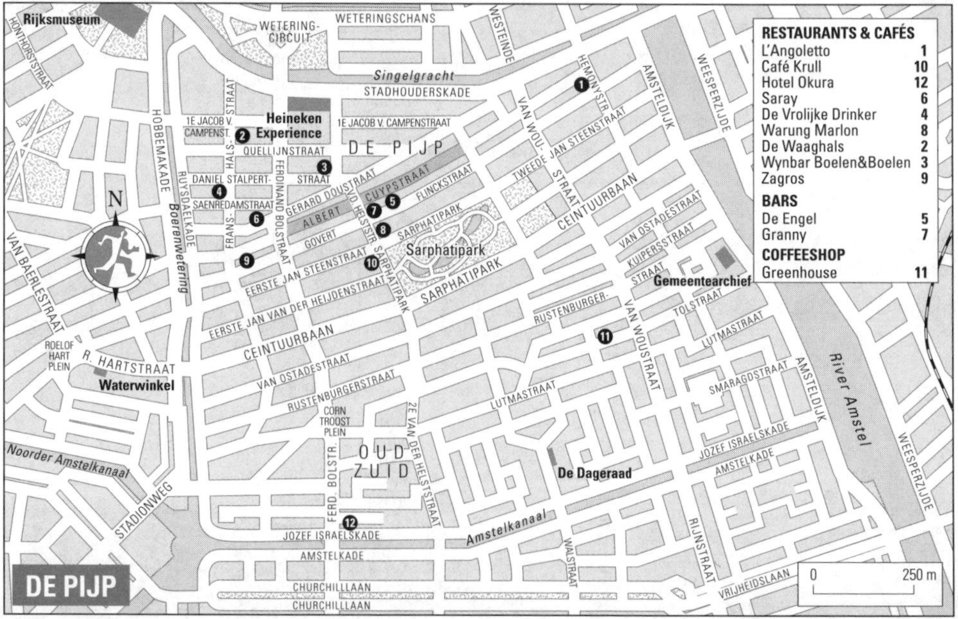
RESTAURANTS & CAFÉS
L'Angoletto 1
Café Krull 10
Hotel Okura 12
Saray 6
De Vrolijke Drinker 4
Warung Marlon 8
De Waaghals 2
Wynbar Boelen&Boelen 3
Zagros 9
BARS
De Engel 5
Granny 7
COFFEESHOP
Greenhouse 11
0
250 m
DE PIJP
Rijksmuseum
Heineken Experience
Sarphatipark
Gemeentearchief
De Dageraad
Waterwinkel
DE PIJP
OUD ZUID
River Amstel
Singelgracht
Boerenwetering
Amstelkanaal
Noorder Amstelkanaal
N
WETERINGSCHANS
WETERING-CIRCUIT
WESTEINDE
STADHOUDERSKADE
HONTHORSTSTRAAT
HOBBEMAKADE
RUYSDAELKADE
VAN BAERLESTRAAT
STADIONWEG
ROELOF HART PLEIN
R. HARTSTRAAT
1E JACOB V. CAMPENST.
1E JACOB V. CAMPENSTRAAT
HALS-STRAAT
QUELLIJNSTRAAT
DANIEL STALPERT-STRAAT
SAENREDAMSTRAAT
FRANS-
FERDINAND BOLSTRAAT
GERARD DOUSTRAAT
ALBERT CUYPSTRAAT
FLINCKSTRAAT
GOVERT
VD. HELSTSTR.
SARPHATIPARK
EERSTE JAN STEENSTRAAT
EERSTE JAN VAN DER HEIJDENSTRAAT
CEINTUURBAAN
VAN OSTADESTRAAT
RUSTENBURGERSTRAAT
CORN TROOST PLEIN
FERD. BOLSTR.
2E VAN DER HELSTSTRAAT
JOZEF ISRAELSKADE
AMSTELKADE
CHURCHILLLAAN
HEMONYSTR.
VAN WOU-STRAAT
TWEEDE JAN STEENSTRAAT
AMSTELDIJK
WEESPERZIJDE
KUIPERSSTRAAT
RUSTENBURGER-STRAAT
TOLSTRAAT
LUTMASTRAAT
VAN WOUSTRAAT
SMARAGDSTRAAT
WALSTRAAT
RIJNSTRAAT
VRIJHEIDSLAAN

▲ HEINEKEN EXPERIENCE

Experience. The brewery was Heineken's headquarters from 1864 to 1988, when the company was restructured and brewing was moved to a more efficient location out of town. Since then, Heineken has developed the site as a tourist attraction with displays on the history of beer-making in general and Heineken in particular. The old brewing facilities are included on the tour, but for many the main draw is the free beer you get to quaff at the end in the bar – three drinks, and a souvenir glass, which isn't bad value.

Albert Cuypstraat market

Ferdinand Bolstraat, running north–south, is De Pijp's main street, but the long, slim east–west thoroughfare of Albert Cuypstraat is its heart. The daily general market held here – which stretches for over a kilometre between Ferdinand Bolstraat and Van Woustraat – is the largest in the city, with a huge array of stalls selling everything from cut-price carrots and raw-herring sandwiches to saucepans and Day-Glo thongs. Check out, too, the bargain-basement and ethnic shops that flank the market on each side, and the Indian and Surinamese restaurants down the side streets – they're often cheaper than their equivalents in the city centre.

The Sarphatipark

Leafy Sarphatipark provides a welcome splash of greenery amongst the surrounding brick and concrete. The park, complete with footpaths and a sinewy lake, was laid out before the construction of De Pijp got underway, and was initially intended as a place for the bourgeoisie to take a picnic.

The Nieuw Zuid

Southwest of De Pijp, the Nieuw Zuid (New South) was the first properly planned extension to the city since the concentric canals of the seventeenth century. The Dutch architect Hendrik Petrus Berlage was responsible for the overall plan, but much of the implementation passed to a pair of prominent architects of the Amsterdam School, Michael de Klerk and Piet Kramer, and it's the playful architectural vision of these two – turrets and bulging windows, sloping roofs and frilly balustrades – that you see in the buildings of the Nieuw Zuid today. As a result, the Nieuw Zuid has become one of Amsterdam's most sought-after addresses. Apollolaan and, a little way to the east, Churchilllaan, are especially favoured and home to some of the city's most sumptuous properties – huge idiosyncratic mansions set back from the street behind trees and generous gardens. Locals pop to the shops on Beethovenstraat, the main drag running south right through the district, and stroll through the languid greenery of the Beatrixpark, or, slightly further out, the Amsterdamse Bos, but there's not much to attract the visitor who isn't a student of modern architecture.

The Amsterdam Hilton

One historic footnote that might entice you this far south is the Amsterdam Hilton, at Apollolaan 138, where John Lennon and Yoko Ono staged their famous week-long "Bed-In" for peace in 1969. Part celebrity farce, part skilful publicity stunt, the couple's anti-war proclamations were certainly heard far and wide, but in Britain the press focused on the supposed evil influence of Yoko on John, which satisfied at least three subtexts – racism, sexism and anti-Americanism.

The Amsterdamse Bos

Ⓦwww.amsterdamsebos.nl. With ten square kilometres of wooded parkland, the Amsterdamse Bos (Amsterdam Forest), to the southwest of the Nieuw Zuid, is the city's largest open space. Planted during the 1930s, the park was a large-scale attempt to provide gainful work for the city's unemployed. Originally a bleak area of flat and marshy fields, it combines a rural feel with that of a well-tended city park – and thus the "forest" tag is something of a misnomer. In the north of the Bos, the Bosbaan is a kilometre-long dead-straight canal, popular for boating and swimming, and there are children's playgrounds and spaces for various sports, including ice skating. There's also a goat farm (Ⓣ020/645 5034) and a nature reserve just to the south with bison and sheep. Canoes and pedaloes can be rented west of the Bosbaan at Grote Vijver ("big pond"; daily April–Oct 10.30am–7.30pm; Ⓣ020/645 7831), or you can simply walk or jog your way around a choice of six clearly marked trails. The new **Bezoekerscentrum het Bosmuseum** (daily noon–5pm; free; Ⓣ020/545 6100), also beside the Bosbaan, at the main entrance to the Bos at Bosbaanweg 5, is a visitor information centre that provides maps and information on the park's facilities, as well as a kids' corner, and upstairs has an exhibition on its history and function. Further information and a map can be found at Boerderij Meerzicht, a first-rate pancake house located to the east of the Bosbaan at Koenenkade 56 (Ⓣ020/679 2744).

▼ THE AMSTERDAM HILTON

The main entrance to the Bos is close to the junction of Amstelveenseweg and Van Nijenrodeweg, some 3km south of the west end of the Vondelpark (for more on which see p.132). **Buses** #170, #171 and #172, departing Centraal Station and the Leidseplein, ply Amstelveenseweg; from the nearest bus stop (Van Nijenrodeweg) it's about 350m to the east end of Bosbaan, where you can rent a bike (April–Oct ☎020/644 5473) – much the best way of getting around.

CoBrA Museum

Sandbergplein, Amstelveen; tram #5 from Centraal Station ☎020/5475050, ⓦwww.cobra-museum.nl. Tues–Sun 11am–5pm. €7.50 5–16-year olds €3.50. A great modern building housing works from the influential CoBrA movement, well worth the trip out. Decent temporary exhibitions too.

The Muiderpoort

Amsterdam East begins with Amsterdam's old eastern gate, the Muiderpoort, a Neoclassical affair complete with a flashy cupola and grandiosely carved pediment. Napoleon staged a triumphal entry into the city through here in 1811, but his imperial pleasure was tempered by his half-starved troops, who could barely be restrained from helping themselves in a city of (what was to them) amazing luxury.

The Tropenmuseum

Linnaeusstraat 2; tram #9 from Centraal Station ☎020/568 8215, ⓦwww.tropenmuseum.nl. Daily 10am–5pm. €7.50, 6- to 17-year-olds €3.75. Despite its general lack of appeal, the East district does have one obvious attraction – the Tropenmuseum, perched on the corner of another of the city's municipal green spaces, the Oosterpark. With its cavernous central hall and three floors of gallery space, this museum has room to focus on themes such as the world's cultural and historical influences, and impresses with its applied art.

▲ THE TROPENMUSEUM

The first floor is dedicated to Dutch colonialism, focusing on Indonesia and the Pacific, with many treasures on show for the first time after having been hidden away for years. Amongst the artefacts, there are Javanese stone friezes, elaborate carved wooden boats from New Guinea, life-size figures dressed in colonial dress and, perhaps strangest of all, ritual ancestor "bispoles" cut from giant New Guinea mangroves. The collection is imaginatively presented in a variety of media – slides, DVDs and sound recordings – and there are also creative and engaging displays devoted to such subjects as music-making and puppetry, as well as traditional storytelling. In addition, there are reconstructions, down to sounds and smells, of typical streets in Iran and Latin America and these aim to provide candid expositions on the problems besetting the world, both culturally – with the year-long exhibition "Urban Islam" – and environmentally.

While you're here, be sure to

look in on the bookshop, which has a good selection of titles on the developing world, and try the inexpensive restaurant, the *Ekeko*, which serves tropical snacks and lunches, including popular national dishes from the exhibited countries. Downstairs, the Tropen Instituut Theater specializes in Third World cinema, music and dance.

Shops

Waterwinkel

Roelof Hartstraat 10 (Oud Zuid) ⊕020/675 5932. The only thing on offer here is water – over 100 different types of bottled mineral water from all over the world. Try the wonderful German *Statl Fasching*.

Coffeeshops

Greenhouse

Tolstraat 91. Consistently sweeps the boards at the annual Cannabis Cup, with medals for its dope as well as "Best Coffeeshop". Tolstraat is a way down to the south (tram #4), but worth the trek: if you're only buying once, buy here. Also branches nearer to the centre at Waterlooplein 345 and O.Z. Voorburgwal 191.

Cafés and tearooms

Granny

1e van der Helststraat 45. Just off the Albert Cuyp market, this café serves up terrific *appelgebak* and *koffie verkeerd*.

Molenaur Vishandel

Albert Cuypstraat 93. What better place to round off your visit to the market than to sample the delights of this excellent – and typical – Dutch fish stall.

Restaurants

L'Angoletto

Hemonystraat 2 ⊕020/676 4182. Closed Sat. Just about everyone's favourite Italian, inexpensive and always packed, with long wooden tables and benches that create a very sociable atmosphere. Not everything they serve is shown on the menu, so keep an eye on the glass showcase in front of the kitchen for any specials. No bookings, so just turn up and hope for the best.

Hotel Okura

Ferdinand Bolstraat 333 ⊕020/678 7111. The two restaurants in this five-star hotel – the sushi restaurant *Yamazato*, and the grill-plate restaurant *Teppan-Yaki Sazanka* – serve the finest Japanese cuisine in the city. Reckon on at least €50 per person. Advance booking essential.

Saray

Gerard Doustraat 33 ⊕020/671 9216. Excellent Turkish eatery down in the De Pijp neighbourhood. Popular with students.

Warung Marlon

1e van der Helststraat 55 ⊕020/671 1526. Daily except Tues 11am–8pm. Surinamese takeaway and popular hangout for lunch, rapidly gaining a loyal clientele. Lively atmosphere.

De Waaghals

Frans Halsstraat 29 ⊕020/679 9609. Tues–Sun 5–9.30pm. Well-prepared organic dishes in this cooperative-run restaurant near the Albert Cuyp.

Zagros

Albert Cuypstraat 50 ⓣ020/670 0461. Popular no-frills Kurdish restaurant run by four brothers. Serves inexpensive traditional dishes from around €3 for starters and €11 for lamb and chicken mains. Vegetarian food available too.

Bars

De Engel

Albert Cuypstraat 182. Excellent spot if you're hankering after a sit-down while you're shopping in the adjacent market. This is a beautifully restored café with huge candle-lit tables and angels painted on the wall. Live jazz on Sat & Sun, and classical music concerts provided on Sunday mornings by local students.

Café Krull

Sarphatipark 2. On the corner of 1e van der Helststraat, a few metres from the Albert Cuyp, this is an atmospheric and lively place. The actual *krull* (curve) is the nearby men's urinoir – designed in a curve. Drinks and snacks all day long from 11am.

East of Eden

Linnaeusstraat 11. A wonderfully relaxed little place right near the Tropenmuseum. Appealing combination of high-ceilinged splendour and gently waving palm trees, with James Dean thrown in to boot. A good way to spend a sunny afternoon.

De Vrolijke Drinker

Frans Halsstraat 66A ⓣ020/771 4316. Mon–Thurs 4pm–1am, Fri & Sat 4pm–3am. One of the more intimate bars along this road, with board games and a large selection of rum. Frequented by

▼ DE ENGEL

▲ EAST OF EDEN

locals and expats alike, friends of the English-speaking owner. From March to November the pavement tables become a pleasant terrace for people-watching.

Wynbar Boelen&Boelen

Eerste van der Helststraat 50 ⓣ020/671 2242. Tues–Sun 5pm–1am. Tasteful wine bar close to Albert Cuypstraat market with a huge selection of wines from around the world, all available by the glass. A heated terrace provides alfresco eating even in the cooler months, and the French restaurant offers seafood delights such as a dozen oysters for around €10.

Clubs and venues

Arena

's-Gravensandestraat 51 ⓣ020/850 2400, ⓦwww.hotelarena.nl. Hip club adjoining a hotel that used to be an orphanage and an asylum. Open Fridays and Saturdays 11pm–4am, with occasional Salsa nights and special parties hosted on a Sunday. International DJs sometimes drop by – and that's when you can expect the entrance fee to jump from around €11 to €20. Tram #6 from Centraal Station.

Day-trips from Amsterdam

Amsterdammers will tell you that there's nothing remotely worth seeing outside their own city, but that's far from the truth. The fast and efficient Dutch railway network puts a whole swathe of the Netherlands within easy reach, including all of the Randstad, a sprawling conurbation that stretches south and east of Amsterdam and encompasses the country's other big cities, The Hague, Utrecht and Rotterdam. Close to Amsterdam, amidst this urban pile-up, Haarlem's attractive centre is home to the outstanding Frans Hals Museum, and is also near the showcase of the country's flower growers, the Keukenhof Gardens. To the north of Amsterdam, the most obvious targets are the old seaports bordering the freshwater Ijsselmeer and Markermeer lakes, formerly – before the enclosing dykes were put in – the choppy and notoriously unpredictable saltwater Zuider Zee. No trains venture out along this coast, but it's an easy bus ride from Amsterdam to the most interesting of them, the former fishing village of Marken, as well as to the beguiling one-time shipbuilding centre of Edam. Edam is, of course, famous for its cheese, but its open-air cheese market is not a patch on that of Alkmaar, an amiable small town forty minutes by train north from Amsterdam. On the way, most trains pause at Koog-Zaandijk, the nearest station to the windmills and canals of the recreated Dutch village of Zaanse Schans, which illustrates eighteenth-century rural life.

Haarlem and the Frans Hals Museum

An easy fifteen-minute journey by train (4 hourly) from Amsterdam's Centraal Station, Haarlem has a very different pace and feel from its big-city neighbour. Once a flourishing cloth-making centre, nowadays it's an easily absorbed town of around 15,000 souls with a good-looking centre studded with fine old buildings. The real draw, however, is the outstanding Frans Hals Museum, located in the almshouse where the artist spent his last, and for some his most brilliant, years. Located at Groot Heiligland 62 (Tues–Sat 11am–5pm, Sun noon–5pm; €5.40; www.franshalsmuseum.nl), it's a five-minute stroll south from the main square, the Grote Markt – take pedestrianized Lange Veerstraat and keep straight as far as Gasthuispoort,

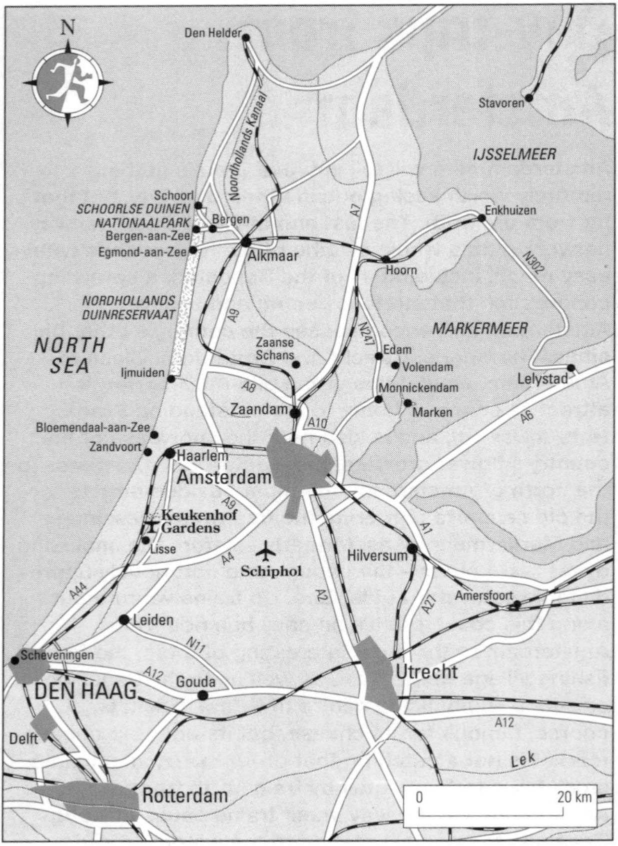

where you turn right and then first left.

The museum holds a relatively small but eclectic collection of Dutch paintings from the fifteenth century onwards and features a handful of prime works by Hals. Chief among the paintings not by Hals are works by Jan van Scorel; Karel van Mander, the leading light of the Haarlem School and mentor of many of the city's most celebrated painters; Haarlem-born Jan Mostaert; and Cornelis Cornelisz van Haarlem. As for Hals, the museum's collection includes the set of "Civic Guard" portraits with which he made his name. Displayed all together, these make a powerful impression – alongside the artist's later, darker works, the most notable of which are the twin *Regents* and *Regentesses of the Oudemannenhuis*. There are those who claim Hals had lost his touch by the time he painted these pictures, yet the sinister, almost ghostly power of the regents facing each other across the room suggests quite the

▲ FRANS HALS MUSEUM

opposite. And Van Gogh's remark that "Frans Hals had no fewer than 27 blacks" suddenly makes perfect sense.

The Keukenhof Gardens

Ⓦ www.keukenhof.com. Late March to late May daily 8am–7.30pm. €12.

The pancake-flat fields extending south from Haarlem towards Leiden are the heart of the Dutch **bulbfields**, whose bulbs and blooms support a billion-dollar industry and some ten thousand growers, as well as attracting tourists in their droves. The small town of Lisse, halfway between Leiden and Haarlem, is home to the Keukenhof Gardens, the largest flower gardens in the world. Literally the "kitchen garden", its site is the former estate of a fifteenth-century countess, who used to grow herbs and vegetables for her dining table here. Some seven million flowers are on show for their full flowering period, complemented, in case of especially harsh winters, by 5000 square metres of glasshouses holding indoor displays. You could easily spend a whole day here, swooning among the sheer abundance of it all, but to get the best of it you need to come early, before the tour buses pack the place. There are several restaurants in the 28 hectares of grounds, and well-marked paths take you all the way through the gardens, which specialize in daffodils, hyacinths and tulips.

To get to the Keukenhof by public transport from Amsterdam (or Haarlem), take the train to Leiden (every 20min) and then catch bus #54 (every 30min) from the adjacent bus station.

Marken

Stuck out in the freshwater Markermeer, the tiny little island of Marken was, until its road connection to the mainland in 1957, pretty much a closed community, supported by a small fishing industry. Nowadays, the fishing has all but disappeared, though the island – or rather its one and only village, Marken – does attract hundreds of day-trippers on account of the picturesque charm of its immaculately maintained houses, mostly painted in deep green with white trimmings, clustered on top of artificial mounds first raised to protect the islanders from the sea. There are two main parts to the village, beginning with **Havenbuurt**, behind the harbour, where the waterfront is dotted with snack bars and souvenir shops, often staffed by locals in traditional costume. The other part – **Kerkbuurt** – centred on the church, is a good deal quieter, its narrow lanes lined by ancient dwellings and old eel-smoking houses. One or two of the houses are open to visitors, proclaiming themselves to be typical of Marken, and here and there you'll find poignant reminders of just how hard life used to be in communities like this.

Marken is accessible direct from Amsterdam on bus #111, departing from outside Centraal Station (every 15–30min; 30min). The bus drops passengers beside the car park on the edge of Marken village, from where it's a five-minute walk to the centre.

Edam

Located just 12km or so up along the coast from Marken, you might expect Edam to be jammed with tourists considering the international fame of the rubbery red balls of cheese that carry its name. In fact, Edam usually lacks the crowds and remains a delightful, good-looking and prosperous little town of neat brick houses, swing bridges and slender canals. In fact, "Edam" is the name of a type of cheese and not its place of origin, and the red balls are produced all over the place, not necessarily even in Holland. Nonetheless the open-air cheese **market** here, held every Wednesday morning in July and August on the Kaasmarkt (10.30am–12.30pm), draws huge crowds.

Leaving Amsterdam every half hour from outside Centraal Station, bus #110 takes 40 minutes to reach Edam. Edam's bus

▼ EDAM MARKET

station is on the southwest edge of town, on Singelweg, a five-minute walk from Damplein. There are no signs, but aim for the easily spotted Speeltoren tower: cross the distinctive swing bridge, turn right and follow Lingerzijde as it jinks left and right. From the Speeltoren, it's a few metres east to the Damplein, where the VVV issues town maps and has details of boat trips both along the local canals and out into the Markermeer. Bike rental is available at Ronald Schot, in the town centre at Grote Kerkstraat 7 (☎029/937 2155, Ⓦwww.ronaldschot.nl); day rental costs €6.50.

Zaanse Schans

April–Oct daily (some parts closed Mon); Nov–March Sat & Sun. Precise times available from the visitor centre, daily 8.30am–5pm ☎075/616 8218, Ⓦwww.zaanseschans.nl. Local trains heading north from Amsterdam's Centraal Station cut through the city's sprawling suburbs en route to **Koog-Zaandijk**, the nearest station to the recreated Dutch village of Zaanse Schans, about 800m away. Made up of around twenty five cottages, windmills and workshops assembled from all over the region, this represents an energetic attempt to reproduce a Dutch village as it would have looked in the eighteenth and early nineteenth century. Spread over a network of narrow canals beside the River Zaan, it's a pretty spot and deservedly popular, with the particular highlight being its string of working windmills, giant industrial affairs used – amongst other things – to cut wood, grind mustard seeds and produce oil. This is the closest place to Amsterdam to see working windmills and there's a scattering of other attractions too, notably a bakery, the inevitable cheese-making workshop and a clog-making workshop. It's actually possible to walk round Zaanse Schans at any time, and in the evening or early morning you may well have the place pretty much to yourself. Finally, there are also enjoyable hour-long **boat trips** on the River Zaan from the jetty near the De Huisman mustard windmill (April–Oct daily 11am–4pm, every hour; €7; ☎075/614 6762).

Alkmaar cheese market

Mid-April to mid-Sept Fri 10am–noon. Forty minutes from Amsterdam by train – and thirty from Koog-Zaandijk (see above) – the little town of Alkmaar was founded in the tenth century in the middle of a marsh. It takes its name from the auk, a diving bird which once hung around here in numbers, as in *alkeen meer*, or auk lake. The town's agreeable, partially canalized centre is still surrounded by its moat, and holds a cluster of impressive medieval buildings, but Alkmaar is perhaps best known for its much-touted **cheese market**, an ancient affair that these days ranks as one of the most extravagant tourist spectacles in Holland. Cheese has been sold on the main square – the Waagplein – since the 1300s, and although it's no longer a serious commercial concern, the market remains popular and continues to draw the crowds. If you want a good view be sure to get here early, as by opening time the crowds are already thick on the ground. The ceremony starts with the buyers sniffing, crumbling, and finally tasting each cheese, followed by intensive bartering. Once a deal has been concluded, the cheeses – golden discs of Gouda mainly, laid out in rows and piles on the square – are borne away on ornamental carriers by groups of four porters for weighing. The porters wear white trousers and shirt plus a black hat whose coloured bands – green, blue, red or yellow – represent the four companies that comprise the cheese porters' guild. Payment for the cheeses, tradition has it, takes place in the cafés around the square.

From Alkmaar's train and bus station, it's about ten minutes' walk to the centre of town: keep straight outside the station along Spoorstraat, take the first right down Snaarmanslaan and then left at busy Geesterweg, which leads over the old city moat to St Laurenskerk. From the church, it's another five minutes' walk east along Langestraat to the VVV (tourist office), housed in the Waag on Waagplein.

Restaurants

Het Hof van Alkmaar

Hof van Sonoy 1, Alkmaar ☎072/512 1222. Occupies delightful premises just off Nieuwesloot. During the day this restaurant offers inexpensive sandwiches, snacks and pancakes, and at night they serve up tasty Dutch cuisine – it's the best place in town.

Restaurant La Plume

Lange Veerstraat 1, Haarlem ☎023/531 3202. A popular and very affordable restaurant with a range of tasty dishes from pastas through to traditional Dutch.

Cafés and bars

Café 1900

Barteljorisstraat 10, Haarlem. With an attractive early twentieth-century interior, this has long been a popular café-bar, serving drinks and light meals.

Proeflokaal 't Apothekertje

Vismarkt, Alkmaar. An old-style bar, open till 2am, with an attractive antique-cluttered interior and a laid-back atmosphere.

▼ CAFÉ 1900

Accommodation

Accommodation

Hotels

Hotel accommodation in Amsterdam can be difficult to find, and is often a major expense, especially in the summer. The city's compactness means that you'll almost inevitably end up somewhere central, but if you arrive without a reservation you'll still need to search hard to find somewhere decent. At peak times of the year – July and August, Easter and Christmas – you'd be advised to book well ahead; hotel rooms can be swallowed up remarkably quickly. You can do this direct or through the **Netherlands Reservations Centre** (ⓣ0031/299 689 144, ⓕ0031/299 689 154, ⓦwww.hotelres.nl) or ⓦwww.bookings.nl, both of which allow you to view availability and prices before making a booking.

Once you've arrived, the city's VVVs (tourist offices) will make hotel reservations on your behalf either in advance or on the same day for a €4 fee, but note that during peak periods and weekends they get extremely busy with long and exhausting queues. There are always loads of people around Centraal Station touting accommodation, and although most of them are genuine enough, the best advice is to steer clear.

Aside from a couple of ultra-cheap places, most hotels start at €65–85 for a double, and some form of breakfast – "Dutch" (bread and jam) or "English" (eggs) – is normally included in the price at all but the cheapest and the most expensive places. A number of hotels have large three- or four-bed family rooms available from €150. Most hotel prices include tax, but some of the more expensive places charge five percent on top of quoted prices.

The Old Centre

The Crown Oudezijds Voorburgwal 21 ⓣ020/626 9664, ⓦwww.hotelthecrown.com. Friendly hotel overlooking a canal. Rooms with large twin beds from €45 per person, without breakfast. Triples, quads and six-person rooms also available, some with a view. Two-night minimum stay at weekends. Safe, despite the location. Late bar until 3am; 3min from CS.

De Gerstekorrel Damstraat 22–24 ⓣ020/624 9771, ⓦwww.gerstekorrel.com. Simple hotel steps away from the Dam, with pleasant staff and large, brightly decorated and well-lit rooms for €135 including buffet breakfast, but on a busy street, so ask for a back room. No lift. Tram #4, #9, #16, #24 or #25 to Dam square.

The Globe Oudezijds Voorburgwal 3 ⓣ020/421 7424, ⓔinfo@hotel-theglobe.nl. A popular hotel and sports-screen bar, which is a favourite with those on all-day drinking binges. In addition to rooms (a steep €95 for a twin) they have dorm beds from €20, €25 on the weekend. Breakfast is extra from €4.50; 5min from CS.

Grand Oudezijds Voorburgwal 197 ⓣ020/555 3111, ⓦwww.thegrand.nl. Originally a Royal Inn dating from 1578, and after that the Amsterdam Town Hall, this fine building is one of the city's architectural high points. The rooms are large and well appointed and decorated in crisp, modern style. All facilities including an inside pool. €420–460 excluding tax and breakfast. Tram #4, #9, #16, #24 or #25 to Dam square.

Grand Hotel Krasnapolsky Dam 9 ⓣ020/554 9111, ⓦwww.nh-hotels.com. Located in a huge and striking mid-nineteenth-century building, this luxurious hotel occupies an entire side of Dam square. If you can't afford the rack-rate (€270 or

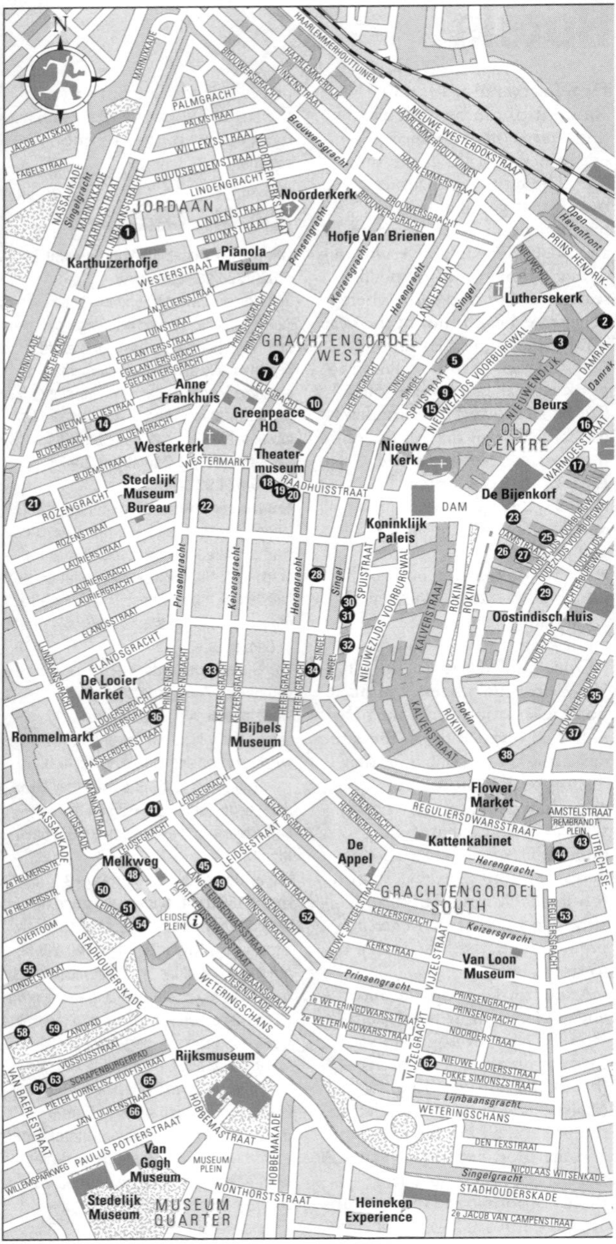
N
JORDAAN
Karthuizerhofje
Pianola Museum
Noorderkerk
Hofje Van Brienen
Luthersekerk
GRACHTENGORDEL WEST
Anne Frankhuis
Greenpeace HQ
Westerkerk
Theater-museum
Stedelijk Museum Bureau
Nieuwe Kerk
Beurs
OLD CENTRE
De Bijenkorf
DAM
Koninklijk Paleis
Oostindisch Huis
De Looier Market
Rommelmarkt
Bijbels Museum
Flower Market
Kattenkabinet
De Appel
GRACHTENGORDEL SOUTH
Melkweg
LEIDSE PLEIN
Van Loon Museum
Rijksmuseum
Van Gogh Museum
MUSEUM PLEIN
Stedelijk Museum
MUSEUM QUARTER
Heineken Experience
HAARLEMMER HOUTTUINEN
BROUWERSGRACHT
HAARLEMMERDIJK
VINKENSTRAAT
NIEUWE WESTERDOKSTRAAT
HAARLEMMERSTRAAT
PALMGRACHT
PALMSTRAAT
WILLEMSSTRAAT
GOUDSBLOEMSTRAAT
LINDENGRACHT
LINDENSTRAAT
BOOMSTRAAT
NOORDERKERKSTRAAT
MARNIXKADE
JACOB CATSKADE
FAGELSTRAAT
NASSAUKADE
Singelgracht
MARNIXSTRAAT
LIJNBAANSGRACHT
Prinsengracht
Keizersgracht
Herengracht
Singel
LANGESTRAAT
Open Havenfront
PRINS HENDRIKKADE
NIEUWENDIJK
DAMRAK
Damrak
WESTERSTRAAT
ANJELIERSSTRAAT
TUINSTRAAT
EGELANTIERSSTRAAT
EGELANTIERSGRACHT
LEIDEGRACHT
NIEUWEZIJDS VOORBURGWAL
SPUISTRAAT
WARMOESSTRAAT
NIEUWE LEIESTRAAT
BLOEMGRACHT
BLOEMSTRAAT
WESTERMARKT
RAADHUISSTRAAT
ROZENGRACHT
ROZENSTRAAT
LAURIERSTRAAT
LAURIERGRACHT
ELANDSSTRAAT
ELANDSGRACHT
DAMSTRAAT
OUDEZIJDS VOORBURGWAL
OUDEZIJDS ACHTERBURGWAL
KALVERSTRAAT
ROKIN
Rokin
KLOVENIERSBURGWAL
LOOIERSGRACHT
PASSEERDERSSTRAAT
LEIDSEGRACHT
LEIDSESTRAAT
REGULIERSDWARSSTRAAT
AMSTELSTRAAT
REMBRANDTPLEIN
UTRECHTSESTRAAT
KERKSTRAAT
NIEUWE SPIEGELSTRAAT
KEIZERSGRACHT
Keizersgracht
REGULIERSGRACHT
1e HELMERSSTR.
2e HELMERSSTR.
LEIDSEKADE
OVERTOOM
STADHOUDERSKADE
VONDELSTRAAT
KORTE LEIDSEDWARSSTRAAT
LANGE LEIDSEDWARSSTRAAT
LIJNBAANSGRACHT
ZIESENISKADE
WETERINGSCHANS
1e WETERINGDWARSSTRAAT
2e WETERINGDWARSSTRAAT
VIJZELSTRAAT
VIJZELGRACHT
PRINSENGRACHT
NOORDERSTRAAT
NIEUWE LOOIERSSTRAAT
FOKKE SIMONSZSTRAAT
Lijnbaansgracht
ZANDPAD
VOSSIUSSTRAAT
SCHAPENBURGERPAD
PIETER CORNELISZ HOOFTSTRAAT
VAN BAERLESTRAAT
JAN LUIJKENSTRAAT
HOBBEMASTRAAT
HOBBEMAKADE
PAULUS POTTERSTRAAT
WILLEMSPARKWEG
NONTHORSTSTRAAT
DEN TEXSTRAAT
NICOLAAS WITSENKADE
Singelgracht
STADHOUDERSKADE
2e JACOB VAN CAMPENSTRAAT
1 2 3 4 5 7 9 10 14 15 16 17 18 19 20 21 22 23 25 26 27 28 29 30 31 32 33 34 35 36 37 38 41 43 44 45 48 49 50 51 52 53 54 55 58 59 62 63 64 65 66

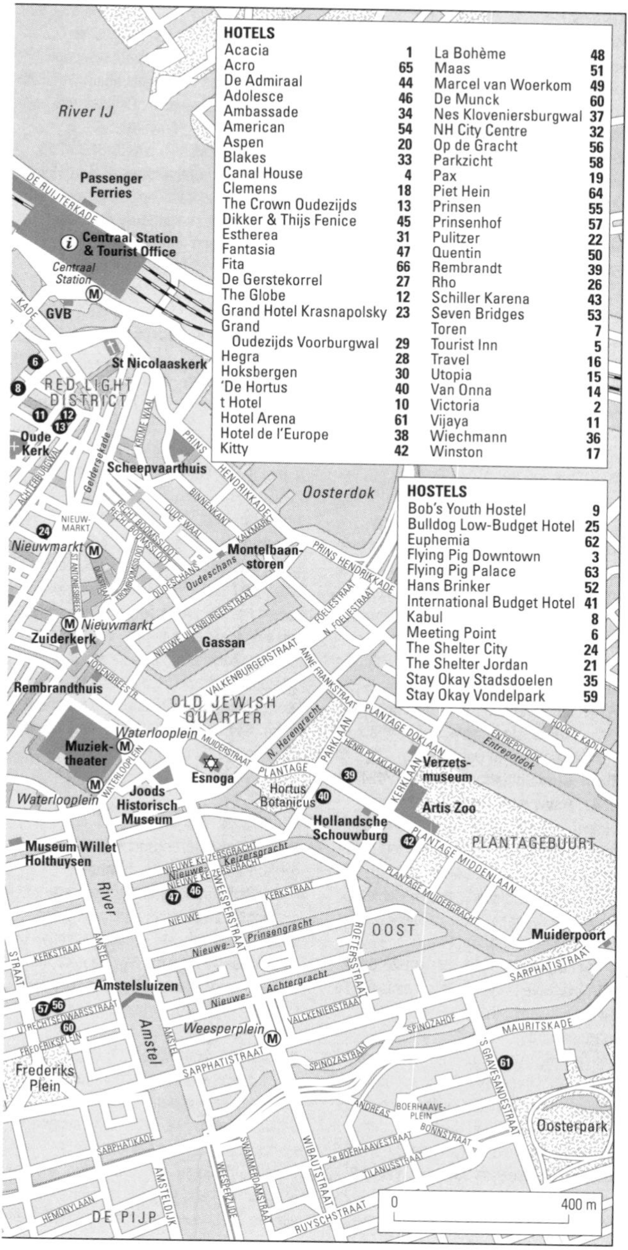

HOTELS

Acacia	1
Acro	65
De Admiraal	44
Adolesce	46
Ambassade	34
American	54
Aspen	20
Blakes	33
Canal House	4
Clemens	18
The Crown Oudezijds	13
Dikker & Thijs Fenice	45
Estherea	31
Fantasia	47
Fita	66
De Gerstekorrel	27
The Globe	12
Grand Hotel Krasnapolsky	23
Grand Oudezijds Voorburgwal	29
Hegra	28
Hoksbergen	30
'De Hortus	40
t Hotel	10
Hotel Arena	61
Hotel de l'Europe	38
Kitty	42
La Bohème	48
Maas	51
Marcel van Woerkom	49
De Munck	60
Nes Kloveniersburgwal	37
NH City Centre	32
Op de Gracht	56
Parkzicht	58
Pax	19
Piet Hein	64
Prinsen	55
Prinsenhof	57
Pulitzer	22
Quentin	50
Rembrandt	39
Rho	26
Schiller Karena	43
Seven Bridges	53
Toren	7
Tourist Inn	5
Travel	16
Utopia	15
Van Onna	14
Victoria	2
Vijaya	11
Wiechmann	36
Winston	17

HOSTELS

Bob's Youth Hostel	9
Bulldog Low-Budget Hotel	25
Euphemia	62
Flying Pig Downtown	3
Flying Pig Palace	63
Hans Brinker	52
International Budget Hotel	41
Kabul	8
Meeting Point	6
The Shelter City	24
The Shelter Jordan	21
Stay Okay Stadsdoelen	35
Stay Okay Vondelpark	59

more for a double), scrape together enough for lunch in the charming Winter Garden, a spectacular atrium in the heart of the hotel. Tram #4, #9, #16, #24 or #25 to Dam square.

Hotel de l'Europe Nieuwe Doelenstraat 2–8 ⓣ020/531 1777, ⓦwww.leurope.nl. Very central hotel which retains a wonderful *fin-de-siècle* charm, with large, well-furnished rooms and a very attractive riverside terrace. Liveried staff and a red carpet on the pavement outside complete the picture. €350 without breakfast and tax. Tram #4, #9, #16, #24 or #25 to Muntplein.

Nes Kloveniersburgwal 137–139 ⓣ020/624 4773, ⓦwww.hotelnes.nl. Extremely pleasant and quiet, with a lift; well positioned away from noise but close to shops and nightlife. Helpful staff. Prices from €150 – they vary depending on the view. Tram #4, #9, #16, #24 or #25 to Muntplein.

Rho Nes 5 ⓣ020/620 7371, ⓦwww.rhohotel.com. A very comfortable hotel in a quiet alley off Dam square that boasts an extraordinary high-ceilinged lounge, originally built as a theatre in 1908. The place looks a bit run-down from the outside, but it's still a good city-centre option, with helpful and welcoming staff. Doubles from €115 including buffet breakfast and tax. Daily bike rental available. Tram #4, #9, #16, #24 or #25 to Dam square.

Tourist Inn Spuistraat 52 ⓣ020/421 5841, ⓦwww.tourist-inn.nl. Popular budget hotel, with clean and comfortable rooms and friendly staff. Six-person dorms with TV (€25), doubles without shower from €80. Triples and quads also available. Considerably higher rates on the weekend. Lift access; 5min from CS.

Travel Beursstraat 23 ⓣ020/626 6532, ⓔinfo@travelhotel.nl. Small, simple hotel on a dingy street that backs onto busy Warmoesstraat. Inside it's very clean and comfortable, with a quiet 24-hour bar and no curfew. Singles and six-bed rooms available, doubles from €80 without bathroom. Light years away from the backpacker places nearby and 10min from CS.

Utopia Nieuwezijds Voorburgwal 132 ⓣ020/626 1295, ⓦwww.hotelutopia.nl. Self-proclaimed "smokers' hotel" above a coffeeshop with tiny, musty rooms over the street, reached by a near-vertical staircase. Basic, and generally welcoming, though there have been complaints about unhelpful staff during peak season. Doubles €60 with shared bathroom. 10min from CS.

Victoria Damrak 1–5 ⓣ020/623 4255, ⓔvicres@parkplazahotels.nl. The *Victoria* is one of the landmarks of the city – a tall, elegant building, wonderfully decorated throughout – and one of the classiest hotels, with every possible amenity. Grimy location, opposite CS. Standard doubles from €300.

Vijaya Oudezijds Voorburgwal 44 ⓣ020/626 9406, ⓦwww.hotelvijaya.com. Stately old canal house in the heart of the Red-Light District, with plain rooms and accommodating management, who also own an Indian restaurant of the same name. En-suite rooms from €95 including breakfast. No lift; 10min from CS.

Winston Warmoesstraat 129 ⓣ020/623 1380, ⓦwww.winston.nl. Popular but noisy hotel designed for an arty crowd. Rooms (sleeping from one to six) are light and airy, some en suite, some with a communal balcony, and many are specially commissioned "art" rooms, including the Durex Room, Heineken Room and Schiffmacher Room. €65 with breakfast. Lift and full disabled access. 10min from CS.

Grachtengordel

De Admiraal Herengracht 563 ⓣ020/626 2150, ⓔde-admiraal-hotel@planet.nl. Friendly hotel close to the nightlife, with wonderful canal views. Breakfast an extra €5. Reception sometimes closes during the day. Doubles from €70 without bathroom, en suite from €98. Quads from €180. Tram #4, #9 or #14 to Rembrandtplein.

Ambassade Herengracht 341 ⓣ020/555 0222, ⓦwww.ambassade-hotel.nl. Elegant canalside hotel made up of ten seventeenth-century houses, with elegant furnished lounges, a well-stocked library and comfortable en-suite rooms from €165. Friendly staff and free 24-hour Internet access. Breakfast is an extra €16, but well worth it. Family rooms from €340. Tram #1, #2 or #5 to Spui.

American Leidsekade 97 ⓣ020/556 3000, ⓦwww.amsterdam-american.crowneplaza.com. Landmark Art Deco hotel dating from 1902 (and in pristine, renovated condition), right on Leidseplein and the water. Large, double-glazed, modern doubles from around €140, with triples also available. Rates exclude tax and breakfast. Tram #1, #2 or #5 from CS to Leidseplein.

Blakes Keizersgracht 384 ⓣ020/530 2010, ⓦwww.blakes-amsterdam.com. The latest Anouchka Hempel hotel (following the well-established one in London), housed in a seventeenth-century building, centred on a beautiful courtyard and terrace. Both the decor and the restaurant menu combine Oriental and European styles. Each of the 41 hip but unpretentious rooms is opulently decorated, featuring exposed beams and natural fabrics. Luxury suites overlook the Keizersgracht canal. Doubles from €390. Tram #1, #2 or #5 from CS to Keizersgracht.

Dikker & Thijs Fenice Prinsengracht 444 ⓣ020/620 1212, ⓦwww.dtfh.nl. Small and stylish hotel on a beautiful canal close to all the shops. Rooms vary in decor but all include a minibar, telephone and TV – those on the top floor give a good view of the city. Standard doubles from €245. Tram #1, #2 or #5 to Prinsengracht.

Estherea Singel 303–309 ⓣ020/624 5146, ⓦwww.estherea.nl. Chic, standard-issue hotel converted from a couple of canal houses. Great location and, although the rooms lack the personal touch, they are all perfectly adequate; the best overlook the canal. €237 excluding tax and breakfast. Tram #1, #2 or #5 from CS to Spui.

Hegra Herengracht 269 ⓣ020/623 7877, ⓦwww.hegrahotelamsterdam.com. Welcoming atmosphere and relatively inexpensive for the location, on a beautiful stretch of the canal. Rooms are small but comfortable; a few have a private bath instead of a shower. Doubles from €65 with breakfast. Tram #1, #2 or #5 to Spui.

Hoksbergen Singel 301 ⓣ020/626 6043, ⓦwww.hotelhoksbergen.nl. Friendly, standard-issue hotel, with a light and open breakfast room overlooking the canal. Basic en-suite rooms, all with telephone and TV, from €85 for smallest room to larger doubles for €104. Breakfast and tax included. Self-catering apartments also available. Tram #1, #2 or #5 from CS to Spui.

La Bohème Marnixstraat 415 ⓣ020/624 2828, ⓦwww.labohemeamsterdam.com. One of the best of the many, many hotels spreading up the Marnixstraat from Leidseplein, this small establishment with super-friendly staff has bright en-suite doubles for €100. Tram #1, #2 or #5 from CS to Leidseplein.

Maas Leidsekade 91 ⓣ020/623 3868, ⓦwww.hemhotels.nl. Another of the well-situated hotels located on this quiet stretch of water, just a short hop from Leidseplein. Modern, clean and well-equipped en-suite rooms – you could ask for one with a waterbed. Double rooms from €145, marginally more for a canal view. Tram #1, #2 or #5 to Leidseplein.

Marcel van Woerkom Leidsestraat 87 ⓣ020/622 9834, ⓦwww.marcelamsterdam.com. Well-known, popular B&B run by an English-speaking graphic designer and artist, who attracts like-minded people to this stylish restored house. Four en-suite doubles available for two, three or four people sharing. Relaxing and peaceful amidst the buzz of the city, with regulars returning year after year, so you'll need to ring well in advance in high season. Breakfast not included, but there are tea- and coffee-making facilities. Rates start at €100 for a double. Tram #1, #2 or #5 to Leidseplein.

De Munck Achtergracht 3 ⓣ020/623 6283, ⓦwww.hoteldemunck.com. Fine, family-run hotel in a quiet spot steps from the Amstel, with clean, light and well-maintained rooms. The Sixties-style breakfast room sports a Wurlitzer jukebox with a good collection of 1960s hits. Doubles €85 including breakfast. Booking recommended. Tram #4 from CS to Frederiksplein.

NH City Centre Spuistraat 288 ⓣ020/420 4545 ⓦwww.nh-hotels.com. Built in the 1920s, this appealing chain hotel occupies an immaculately renovated Art Deco former textile factory. Well-situated for the cafés and bars of the Spui, and the Museum Quarter. Rooms vary in size, some have canal views, and all boast extremely comfy beds and good showers. Doubles from €89, more at weekends. The buffet breakfast is an extra €16, but will set you up for the day. Tram #1, #2 or #5 from CS to Spui.

Op de Gracht Prinsengracht 826 ⓣ020/626 1937, ⓦwww.opdegracht.nl. B&B in a good-looking canal house on one of the main canals, run by the very pleasant Jolanda Schipper. Two rooms tastefully decorated, both with en-suite bathroom. Minimum stay two nights. Doubles €80 & €90. Tram #4 from CS to Prinsengracht.

Prinsenhof Prinsengracht 810 ⓣ020/623 1772, ⓦwww.hotelprinsenhof.com. Tastefully decorated, this is one of the city's top budget options with doubles at €60 without shower. Booking essential. Tram #4 to Prinsengracht.

Pulitzer Prinsengracht 315 ⓣ020/523 5235, ⓦwww.starwood.com. An entire row of seventeenth-century canal houses creatively converted into a five-star chain hotel. Very popular with visiting businessfolk, but although the public areas are tastefully decorated and the breakfasts very good, the modern rooms lack character and some – considering the price – are very disappointing. From €240 for a double. Tram #13 or #17 from CS to Westermarkt.

Quentin Leidsekade 89 ⓣ020/626 2187, ⓕ202/622 0121, ⓦwww.quentinhotels.com. Very friendly small hotel, often a stopover for artists performing at the Melkweg (see p.102). Welcoming to all, but especially well-regarded among gay and lesbian visitors. Double rooms €90, more at weekends. Breakfast of fruit and cereal extra €7. Tram #1, #2 or #5 to Leidseplein.

Schiller Karena Rembrandtplein 26–36 ⓣ020/554 0700, ⓔnhschiller@nh-hotels.com. Once something of a hangout for Amsterdam's intellectuals, the *Schiller* still has one of the city's better-known and more atmospheric bars on its ground floor. Named after the renowned painter and architect, whose works are liberally sprinkled throughout the hotel. Fetching Art Deco furnishings in all the public areas. The drawback is its location – on tacky Rembrandtplein. Rates begin at about €200 per double without breakfast. Tram #4, #9 or #14 to Rembrandtplein.

Seven Bridges Reguliersgracht 31 ⓣ020/623 1329. Perhaps the city's most charming hotel – and certainly one of its better-value ones. Takes its name from its canalside location, which affords a view of no less than seven dinky little bridges. Beautifully decorated, its spotless rooms are regularly revamped. Rates start at €100 per double, and vary with the view. Small and popular, so often booked solid. Breakfast is served in your room. Tram #4 or #9 to Prinsengracht.

Wiechmann Prinsengracht 328–332 ⓣ020/626 3321, ⓦwww.hotelwiechmann.nl. Canal-house restoration, family-run for fifty years, with dark wooden beams and restrained style throughout. Large, bright rooms in perfect condition with TV and shower cost €120. Close to the Anne Frank House. Prices stay the same throughout the year. Tram #13 or #17 from CS to Westermarkt.

Western canals and the Jordaan

Acacia Lindengracht 251 ⓣ020/622 1460, ⓔacacia.nl@wxs.nl. Well-kept hotel, situated right on a corner, so some of the rooms have wide views of the canal and its adjoining streets. There are also self-catering apartments. Doubles from €80 including breakfast; three-, four- and five-bed rooms too. A 15-minute walk from CS.

Aspen Raadhuisstraat 31 ⓣ020/626 6714, ⓦwww.hotelaspen.nl. One of a number of inexpensive hotels situated in the Art Nouveau crescent of the Utrecht Building. Family-run with basic but tidy rooms, which are checked every day. Small doubles €46 or €76 with en suite. No breakfast. Tram #13 or #17 from CS to Westermarkt.

Canal House Keizersgracht 148 ⓣ020/622 5182, ⓦwww.canalhouse.nl. Magnificently restored seventeenth-century building, centrally located on one of the principal canals. Comfortable rooms, but generally brusque staff. Doubles from €150. Tram #13 or #17 from CS to Westermarkt.

Clemens Raadhuisstraat 39 ⓣ020/624

6089, ⓦwww.clemenshotels.nl. Friendly, well-run budget hotel, with knowledgeable owner, close to the Anne Frank House and museums. One of the better options along this busy main road. Individually decorated doubles without shower from €70, with shower €110. Breakfast extra. Prices stay the same throughout the year. All rooms offer free Internet connection, and you can rent laptops for €8. Tram #13 or #17 from CS to Westermarkt.

't Hotel Leliegracht 18 ⓣ020/422 2741, ⓔth.broekema@hetnet.nl. Extremely pleasant hotel located along a quiet canal. Owned by the proprietor of an antique shop, who believes in making people feel at home. Eight spacious rooms, large beds, TV, fridge and either bath or shower. No groups. Minimum three-night stay at the weekend; €134 with breakfast. Tram #13 or #17 from CS to Westermarkt.

Pax Raadhuisstraat 37 ⓣ020/624 9735. Straightforward city-centre cheapie, owned by two brothers. A mixture of fair-sized rooms sleeping one to four persons, but plans are afoot to refurbish the rooms in the minimalist style of room no.19 – the large double on the top floor. In the meantime, as with most of the hotels along this street, ask for a room at the back. Doubles €75 or €90 for three people. Tram #13, #14 or #17 to Westermarkt.

Ramenas Haarlemmerdijk 61 ⓣ020/624 6030, ⓔramenas730@hotmail.com. Welcoming budget hotel that's only recently changed hands, and is run by the owners of the bar downstairs. Large, basic rooms at sensible prices, though those at the front can be a bit noisy. Located to the northwest of the centre, away from the nightlife, but with reasonably good access to the city centre; 15min from CS. Doubles €70 without breakfast.

Toren Keizersgracht 164 ⓣ020/622 6033, ⓦwww.hoteltoren.nl. Fine example of an imaginatively revamped seventeenth-century canal house, once the home of a Dutch prime minister and now popular with American visitors. Opulently designed en-suite doubles with a touch of class from €285. Some deluxe rooms have a Jacuzzi. Friendly and efficient staff. Tram #13 or #17 from CS to Westermarkt.

Van Onna Bloemgracht 102 ⓣ020/626 5801, ⓦwww.vanonna.nl. A quiet, well-maintained, family-run place on a tranquil canal. The building dates back over three hundred years and still retains some of its original fixtures. Simple setup, no TV, no smoking and cash payment only. Rooms sleeping up to four people for €40 per person, including all services. Booking advised. Tram #13 or #17 from CS to Westermarkt.

The Old Jewish Quarter and the East

Adolesce Nieuwe Keizersgracht 26 ⓣ020/626 3959, ⓦwww.adolesce.nl. Popular and welcoming hotel, with ten neat if unspectacular rooms and a large dining room and bar. Closed Oct–April. Doubles €100, triples available. No breakfast. Tram #9 from CS to Waterlooplein.

Fantasia Nieuwe Keizersgracht 16 ⓣ020/623 8259, ⓦwww.fantasia-hotel.com. Nicely situated family-run hotel on a broad, quiet canal just off the Amstel; the rooms are well maintained, connected by quaint, narrow corridors, and there are also some very attractive attic doubles for €84. Triples and a family room also available. Closed Jan–March, and most of Dec. Tram #9 from CS to Waterlooplein.

De Hortus Plantage Parklaan 8 ⓣ020/625 9996, ⓦwww.hotelhortus.com. Smoker-friendly cheapie close to the Hortus Botanicus gardens. Rooms vary in size, from two- to twelve-person, and maintenance is kept to a minimum, but they're clean, and the common room, equipped with free Internet access, pool table and coffee machine, has a good atmosphere. Note that you need to confirm your booking two days prior, otherwise you'll lose the room. All rooms €25 per person. Tram #9 from CS to Artis Zoo.

Hotel Arena 's-Gravesandestraat 51 ⓣ020/850 2410, ⓦwww.hotelarena.nl. A little way east of the centre, in a renovated old convent on the edge of the Oosterpark, this place has been thoroughly revamped, transforming a popular hostel into a hip three-star hotel complete with split-level rooms and minimalist decor. Despite the odd pretentious flourish, it manages to retain a relaxed vibe attracting both businesspeople and travellers alike. Lively bar, intimate restaurant, and late-night club (Fri & Sat) located within the former chapel. Doubles start at €125. Metro Weesperplein, then walk, or take tram #9 from CS to the Tropenmuseum.

Kitty Plantage Middenlaan 40 ⓣ020/622 6819. Located above a butcher's and run by the same person for the past 23 years, this quiet, large old house is a little out from the centre, but in an interesting neighbourhood close to the zoo. Popular with visitors looking for somewhere quiet. Decent-sized rooms from €55 a double. Tram #9 from CS to Plantage Badlaan.

Rembrandt Plantage Middenlaan 17 ⓣ020/627 2714, ⓦwww.hotelrembrandt.nl. Elegant hotel with a dining room dating from the sixteenth century, though the building itself is nowhere near as old. Rooms are decorated in crisp modern style with wood interiors, and all are en suite. Doubles €85 including breakfast. Tram #9 from CS to Artis Zoo. Minimum two-night stay at weekends in high season.

The Museum Quarter and the Vondelpark

Acro Jan Luyckenstraat 44 ⓣ020/662 5538, ⓦwww.acro-hotel.nl. Excellent, modern hotel with stylish rooms, a plush bar and self-service restaurant (breakfast only). Well worth the money; reserve at least two months in advance. Doubles from €95 with breakfast. Tram #2 or #5 from CS to Van Baerlestraat.

AMS Atlas Van Eeghenstraat 64 ⓣ020/676 6336, ⓦwww.ams.nl. Situated near the Vondelpark and occupying an attractive Art Nouveau building, the *Atlas* is a personable modern hotel with every convenience and comfort, plus an à la carte restaurant. Small, tranquil and very welcoming. Rooms start at an affordable €140 with discounts often available too. Tram #2 from CS to Jacob Obrechtstraat.

AMS Hotel Holland P.C. Hooftstraat 162 ⓣ020/676 4253, ⓦwww.ams.nl. Comfortable, quiet and welcoming two-star hotel at the end of the street near the Vondelpark. Doubles from €109. Tram #2 to Van Baerlestraat or #5 to Paulus Potterstraat.

Bema Concertgebouwplein 19b ⓣ020/679 1396, ⓔpostbus@hotel-bema.demon.nl. Large, clean rooms within a huge house under the canny eye of the friendly English-speaking manager-owner. The rooms aren't modern (the beds can be a bit uncomfortable), but they're full of funky character. Handy for concerts and museums. En-suite rooms €85, with breakfast of bread with ham and cheese delivered to your room. Triples, quads and apartments available too. Tram #5 to Museumplein.

Fita Jan Luyckenstraat 37 ⓣ020/679 0976, ⓦwww.fita.nl. Mid-sized, friendly family-run hotel in a quiet spot between the Vondelpark and the museums. Comfortable en-suite doubles from €120 (extra bed €25). All rooms non-smoking. Tram #2 or #5 to Van Baerlestraat.

Parkzicht Roemer Visscherstraat 33 ⓣ020/618 1954, ⓕ020/618 0897. Quiet, unassuming little hotel on a pretty backstreet near the Vondelpark, with an appealingly lived-in look. Clean and characterful, some rooms have fireplaces, and are furnished with old Dutch furniture. En suites from €75, including breakfast. Closed between Nov and March. Tram #1 from CS to 1e Constantijn Huygensstraat.

Piet Hein Vossiusstraat 53 ⓣ020/662 7205, ⓦwww.hotelpiethein.nl. Calm, low-key and stylish, tucked away on a quiet street running past the Vondelpark, midway between Leidseplein and the Concertgebouw. Bar open till 1am. Lift access. Rooms from €140. Tram #1, #2 or #5 from CS to Leidseplein. Recommended.

Prinsen Vondelstraat 38 ⓣ020/616 2323, ⓦwww.prinsenhotel.demon.nl. Family-style hotel on the edge of the Vondelpark; quiet and with a large, secluded back garden. Marginally higher rates at the weekend, otherwise €120 with breakfast. Tram #1 from CS to 1e Constantijn Huygensstraat.

Zandbergen Willemsparkweg 205 ⓣ020/676 9321, ⓦwww.hotel-zandbergen.com. Light, airy, family-run hotel on a busy street near the Vondelpark; the rooms are clean and spacious. Non-smoking rooms from €130. Minimum two-night stay during peak periods. Tram #2 from CS to Emma Street.

Hostels

If you're on a tight budget, the least expensive central option is to take a dormitory bed in a **hostel** – and there are plenty to choose from: Hostelling International places, unofficial private hostels, even Christian hostels. Most hostels will either provide (relatively) clean bed linen or charge a few euros for it, though frankly your own sleeping bag might be a better option. Many hostels also lock guests out for a short period each day to clean the place, and some set a nightly curfew, though these are usually late enough not to cause too much of a problem. Many hostels don't accept reservations from June to August.

The Old Centre

Bob's Youth Hostel **Nieuwezijds Voorburgwal 92 ⓣ020/623 0063, ⓦwww.bobshostel.nl.** An old favourite with backpackers and a grungy crowd, *Bob's* is lively and smoky. Small dorms at €18 per person, including breakfast in the coffeeshop on the ground floor (which does light snacks). They also let four apartments (€70 for two people, €80 for three). However, they kick everyone out at 10.30am to clean, which is not so good if you want a lie-in; 10min from CS.

Bulldog Low-Budget Hotel **Oudezijds Voorburgwal 220 ⓣ020/620 3822, ⓦwww.bulldog.nl.** Part of the Bulldog coffeeshop chain, and recently renovated into "a five-star hotel for backpackers". Bar and DVD lounge downstairs complete with leather couches and soft lighting. Dorm beds with TV and shower start at €26, including breakfast and wake-up service, linen €3 extra. Also double rooms, as well as fully equipped luxury apartments available from €135. Tram #4, #9, #16 or #24 from CS to Dam, then a 3min walk.

Flying Pig Downtown **Nieuwendijk 100 ⓣ020/420 6822, ⓦwww.flyingpig.nl.** Clean, large and well run by ex-travellers familiar with the needs of backpackers. Free use of kitchen facilities, no curfew, and there's a late-night coffeeshop next door. Hostel bar open all night. Justifiably popular, and a very good deal, with dorm beds from just €21 depending on the size of the dorm; queensize bunks sleeping two also available; €10 deposit for sheets and keys. During the peak season you'll need to book well in advance. See also the *Flying Pig Palace*, p.162; 5min from CS.

Kabul **Warmoesstraat 38 ⓣ020/623 7158, ⓔkabulhotel@hotmail.com.** Large and bustling cheapie, open 24 hours, with basic rooms sleeping between one and sixteen people; €22 in peak season, including use of all facilities. Not always as clean as it might be, but there's no lockout or curfew and you can book in advance. Groups welcome; 3min from CS.

Meeting Point **Warmoesstraat 14 ⓣ020/627 7499, ⓔinfo@hostel-meetingpoint.nl.** Warm and cosy central hostel with space in twelve- to eighteen-bed dorms going for €18 per person during the week. Four-person dorms also available from €92. Breakfast of bread, jam and eggs €2.50. Checkout 10am; 24-hour private bar and pool table for guests; 2min from CS.

The Shelter City **Barndesteeg 21 ⓣ020/625 3230, ⓦwww.shelter.nl.** A non-evangelical Christian youth hostel smack in the middle of the Red-Light District. At €18.50 these are some of the best-value beds in Amsterdam, with bed linen, shower and sizeable breakfast included. Dorms are single-sex; lockers require a €5 deposit and there's a midnight curfew (1am at weekends). You might be handed a booklet on Jesus when you check in, but you'll get a quiet night's sleep and the sheets are clean. Metro Nieuwmarkt.

Stay Okay Stadsdoelen **Kloveniersburgwal 97 ⓣ020/624 6832, ⓦwww.stayokay.com/stadsdoelen.** The closest to Centraal Station of the two official hostels, with clean, semi-private dorms at €20 for members, who get priority in high season; non-members pay €22.50. Price includes linen, breakfast and locker, plus use of communal kitchen. Guests get a range of discounts on activities in the city too, and you can also book Eurolines bus tickets here, with card holders receiving a ten-percent discount. The bar overlooks the canal and serves good-value if basic food, and there's a 2am curfew (though the door opens for three 15min intervals between 2am and 7am). Metro Nieuwmarkt, or tram #4, #9, #16, #24 or #25 from CS to Muntplein. The other HI hostel is the *Stay Okay Vondelpark* (see below), which is better equipped for large groups.

Grachtengordel

Euphemia Fokke Simonszstraat 1–9 ⓣ & ⓕ020/622 9045, ⓦwww.euphemiahotel.com. Situated a shortish walk from Leidseplein and the major museums, with a likeable laid-back atmosphere and basic but large rooms. Doubles €78.50, triples from €87 and four-bed rooms for €35 per person, but prices are half that during the low season. Breakfast extra €5. Booking advised. Tram #16, #24 or #25 from CS to Weteringcircuit.

Hans Brinker Kerkstraat 136 ⓣ020/622 0687, ⓕ020/638 2060. Well-established and raucously popular Amsterdam hostel, with 580 beds. Dorm beds go for around €24 including breakfast, and singles, doubles and triples are also available. All rooms en suite. The facilities are good: free Internet after 10pm, disco every night, and dorms are basic and clean – it's near to the buzz of Leidseplein too. A hostel to head for if you're out for a good time (and not too bothered about getting a solid night's sleep), though be prepared to change dorms during your stay. Walk-in policy only. Tram #1, #2 or #5 from CS to Prinsengracht.

International Budget Hotel Leidsegracht 76 ⓣ020/624 2784, ⓔinfo@internationalbudgethostel.com. An excellent budget option on a peaceful little canal in the heart of the city, with the same owners as the *Euphemia* (see above). Small, simple rooms sleeping up to four, with singles and doubles available; twins from €65. Young, friendly staff. Tram #1, #2 or #5 to Prinsengracht.

Western canals and the Jordaan

The Shelter Jordan Bloemstraat 179 ⓣ020/624 4717, ⓦwww.shelter.nl. The second of Amsterdam's two Christian youth hostels (the other is *Shelter City*, see p.161). Great value at €18.50 per dorm bed, with breakfast and bed linen included. Dorms are single-sex, lockers require a €5 deposit and there's a 2am curfew. Friendly and helpful staff, plus a decent café. Sited in a particularly beautiful part of the Jordaan, close to the Lijnbaansgracht canal. Non-smoking rooms. Tram #6, #13 or #17 from CS to Marnixstraat.

The Museum Quarter and the Vondelpark

Flying Pig Palace Vossiusstraat 46 ⓣ020/400 4187, ⓦwww.flyingpig.nl. The better of the two *Flying Pig* hostels, facing the Vondelpark and close to the city's most important museums. Immaculately clean and well maintained by a staff of travellers, who understand their backpacking guests. Free use of kitchen facilities, no curfew and good tourist information. Ten-bed dorms start at €21.70 per person and there are a few two-person queensize bunks at €31.80, as well as double rooms. Great value. Tram #1, #2 or #5 from CS to Leidseplein, then walk.

Stay Okay Vondelpark Zandpad 5 ⓣ020/589 8996, ⓦwww.stayokay.com/vondelpark. Well located and, for facilities, the better of the city's two HI hostels, with a bar, restaurant, TV lounge, Internet access and bicycle shed, plus various discount facilities for tours and museums. HI members have priority in high season and pay €2.50 less than non-members. Non-member rates are €23 per person in the dorms, including use of all facilities, shower, sheets and breakfast. Singles, doubles and rooms sleeping up to eight are available. Secure lockers and no curfew. To be sure of a place in high season you'll need to book at least two months ahead. Tram #1, #2 or #5 from CS to Leidseplein, then walk.

Essentials

Essentials

Arrival

Arriving in Amsterdam by train and plane could hardly be easier. Schiphol, Amsterdam's international **airport**, is a quick and convenient train ride away from Centraal Station, the city's **international train station**, which is itself just a ten-minute metro ride from Amstel Station, the terminus for long-distance and international buses.

By air

Amsterdam's international airport, **Schiphol** (ⓣ0900/7244 7465, ⓦwww.schiphol.nl), is located about 18km southwest of the city centre. Trains run from there to Amsterdam Centraal Station every ten minutes during the day, every hour at night (midnight–6am); the journey takes 15–20 minutes and costs €3.10 each way. The main alternative to the train is the **Airport Hotel Shuttle Bus** (ⓣ020/653 4975), which departs from the designated bus stop outside the Arrivals hall. Most of these buses – but not all – sport a "Connexxion" logo, though otherwise liveries vary; note also that you don't have to be a guest to use them. Departures are every 20–30 minutes from 6am to 8pm and the cost is €10.50, €19 return. The route varies with the needs of the passengers it picks up at the airport, but buses take about thirty minutes to get from the airport to the Old Centre. Finally, the **taxi** fare from Schiphol to the Old Centre is €40–45.

By train

Amsterdam's **Centraal Station** (CS) has regular connections with key cities in Germany, Belgium and France, as well as all the larger towns and cities of the Netherlands. Amsterdam also has several suburban train stations, but these are principally for the convenience of commuters. For all rail enquiries contact **NS** (Netherlands Railways; international enquiries ⓣ0900/9296; domestic enquiries ⓣ0900/9292, ⓦwww.ns.nl).

By bus

Eurolines (ⓣ020/560 8788, ⓦwww.eurolines.nl) long-distance, international buses arrive at Amstel Station, about 3.5km to the southeast of Centraal Station. The metro journey to Centraal Station takes about ten minutes.

Red tape and visas

Citizens of the UK, Ireland, Australia, New Zealand, Canada and the US do not need a **visa** to enter the Netherlands if staying for three months or less. However, citizens of these countries do need to be in possession of a passport valid for at least six months after arrival, as well as a return airline ticket and/or funds deemed to be sufficient to fund their stay.

There are no customs restrictions on importing goods (except tobacco) from another EU country, as long as they are not duty-free and you can prove that the goods are for personal use. If you are arriving in the Netherlands from a non-EU country, the following import limits apply: 200g cigarettes or 250g tobacco, 1 litre of spirits or 2 litres of wine, 50g perfume. If you're caught with more than these amounts, you'll have to pay tax on them, and possibly import duties as well. When you leave the Netherlands, there are no export restrictions on goods if you're travelling on to an EU country, but if you're travelling to a non-EU destination, you will be subject to the import regulations of your destination country. There are no restrictions on the import and export of currency.

City transport

Almost all of Amsterdam's leading attractions are clustered in or near the city centre, within easy walking – and even easier cycling distance of each other. For longer jaunts, the city has a first-rate public transport system, run by the **GVB**, comprising trams, buses, a smallish metro and four passenger ferries across the river IJ to the northern suburbs. Centraal Station is the hub of the system with a multitude of trams and buses departing from outside on Stationsplein, which is also the location of a metro station and a GVB public transport information office. There's a taxi rank on Stationsplein too.

Trams, buses and the metro

The city centre is crisscrossed by **trams**. Two of the more useful are trams #2 and #5, which link Centraal Station with Leidsestraat and the Rijksmuseum every ten minutes or so during the day. **Buses** are mainly useful for going to the outskirts, and the same applies to the **metro**, which has just two downtown stations, Nieuwmarkt and Waterlooplein. Trams, buses and the metro operate daily between 6am and midnight, supplemented by a limited number of nightbuses (*nachtbussen*). All tram and bus stops display a detailed map of the network. For further details on all services, head for the main GVB information office (Mon–Fri 7am–9pm, Sat & Sun 8am–9pm; ⓣ0900/8011, ⓦwww.gvb.nl) on Stationsplein. Their free, English-language *Tourist Guide to Public Transport* is very helpful.

The most common type of **ticket**, usable on all forms of GVB transport, is the **strippenkaart**, a card divided into strips: fold your *strippenkaart* over to expose the number of strips required for your journey and then insert it into the on-board franking machine. Amsterdam's public transport system is divided into zones, and one person making a journey within one zone costs two strips. The "Centre" zone covers the city centre and its immediate surroundings (well beyond Singelgracht), and thus two strips will cover more or less every journey you're likely to make. If you travel into an additional zone, it costs three strips, and so on. More than one person can use a *strippenkaart*, as long as the requisite number of strips is stamped. After franking, you can use any GVB tram, bus and the metro for up to one hour. Currently, a two-strip *strippenkaart* costs €1.60, three-strip €2.40, fifteen-strip €6.40 and a 45-strip €18.90.

You can opt instead for a **dagkaart** (day ticket), which gives unlimited access to the GVB system for up to a maximum of three days. Prices are €6.30 for one day, €10 for two, and €13 for three. Tickets and passes are available from tobacconists, the GVB, the VVV and metro stations; the smaller *strippenkaart* is also available from bus and tram drivers. Finally, note that GVB tries hard to keep fare dodging down to a minimum and wherever you're travelling, and at whatever time of day, there's a reasonable chance you'll have your ticket checked. If you are caught without a valid ticket, you risk an on-the-spot fine of €29.40.

The Canal Bus

One good way to get around Amsterdam's waterways is to take the **Canal Bus** (ⓣ020/623 9886, ⓦwww.canal.nl). This operates on three circular routes, which meet once, at the jetty opposite Centraal Station beside Prins Hendrikkade. Two of the three routes also meet at three other locations – on the Singelgracht (opposite the Rijksmuseum), behind the Leidseplein and beside City Hall on Waterlooplein. There are eleven stops in all and together they give easy access to all the major sights. Boats leave from opposite Centraal Station (every 10–20min; 10am–5.30pm) and at least every half-hour from any other jetty. A day ticket for all three routes, allowing you to hop on and off as many times as you like, costs €15 per adult, €10.50 for children (4–12 years old); it's valid until noon the following day and entitles the bearer to minor discounts at several museums.

The Museumboot

A similar boat service, the **Museumboot** (☎020/530 1090, Ⓦwww.lovers.nl), calls at seven jetties located at or near many of the city's major attractions. It departs from opposite Centraal Station (every 30min; 9.30am–5pm) and a come-and-go-as-you-please day ticket costs €14.25, children €9.50 (4–12 years old).

Canal Bikes

Canal Bikes (☎020/626 5574, Ⓦwww.canal.nl) are four-seater **pedaloes** which take a lifetime to get anywhere but are nevertheless good fun unless – of course – it's raining. You can rent them at four central locations: on the Singelgracht opposite the Rijksmuseum; the Prinsengracht outside the Anne Frank House; on Keizersgracht at Leidsestraat; and behind Leidseplein. Rental prices per person per hour are €7 (3–4 people) or €8 (1–2 people), plus a refundable deposit of €50. They can be picked up at one location and left at any of the others; opening times are daily 10am–6pm, till 9.30pm in July and August.

Bicycles

One of the most agreeable ways to explore Amsterdam is by **bicycle**. The city has an excellent network of designated bicycle lanes (*fietspaden*) and for once cycling isn't a fringe activity – there are cyclists everywhere. Indeed, much to the chagrin of the city's taxi drivers, the needs of the cyclist often take precedence over those of the motorist and by law if there's a collision it's always the driver's fault. Bike rental is straightforward. There are lots of **rental companies** (*fietsenverhuur*) but MacBike (☎020/620 0985, Ⓦwww.macbike.nl) sets the benchmark, charging €4 for two hours, €12 per day, €16.50 for three days and €30 for a week for a standard bicycle; 21-speed cycles cost twice as much. MacBike have three rental outlets in central Amsterdam, one at the east end of Centraal Station, a second beside Waterlooplein at Mr Visserplein 2, and a third near Leidseplein at Weteringschans 2. All companies, including MacBike, ask for some type of security, usually in the form of a cash deposit (some will take credit card imprints) and/or passport.

Taxis

The centre of Amsterdam is geared up for trams and bicycles rather than cars, with motorists having to negotiate a convoluted one-way system, avoid getting boxed onto tram lines and steer round herds of cyclists. As such, **taxis** are not as much use as they are in many other cities. They are, however, plentiful: taxi ranks are liberally distributed across the city centre and they can also be hailed on the street. If all else fails, call the city's central, 24-hour taxi number on ☎020/677 7777. **Fares** are metered and pricey, but distances are small: the trip from Centraal Station to the Leidseplein, for example, costs just €11, €2 more to Museumplein – and about fifteen percent more late at night.

Organized tours

No one could say the Amsterdam tourist industry doesn't make the most of its canals, with a veritable armada of glass-topped **cruise boats** shuttling along the city's waterways, offering everything from quick hour-long excursions to fully-fledged dinner cruises. There are several major operators and they occupy the prime pitches – the jetties near Centraal Station on Stationsplein, beside the Damrak and on Prins Hendrikkade. Despite the competition, **prices** are fairly uniform with a one-hour tour costing around €8.50 per adult, €5.50 per child (4–12 years old), and €25 (€15) for a two-hour candlelit cruise. The big companies also offer more specialized boat trips, most notably the weekly Architecture Cruise run by Lovers

Tour operators

Reederij P. Kooij on the Rokin, beside the Queen Wilhelmina statue ⓣ020/623 3810, ⓦwww.rederijkooij.nl. Perhaps the best of the waterway cruise operators, with a standard range of cruises by day and by night. Also has a (more crowded) jetty opposite Centraal Station on Stationsplein.
Mee in Mokum Keizersgracht 346 ⓣ020/625 1390. Guided walking tours of the older parts of the city provided by long-time – and often older – Amsterdam residents. Tours run four or five times weekly; €3 per person. Advance reservations required.
Yellow Bike Tours Nieuwezijds Kolk 29, off Nieuwezijds Voorburgwal ⓣ020/620 6940, ⓦwww.yellowbike.nl. Three-hour guided cycling tours around the city (April to mid-Oct 2 daily). Tours cost €17 per person, including the bike. Advance reservations required.

(ⓣ020/530 1090, ⓦwww.lovers.nl; €19.50/14.50). All these cruises – and especially the shorter and less expensive ones – are extremely popular and long queues are common throughout the summer. One way of avoiding much of the crush is to walk down the Damrak from Centraal Station to the jetty at the near end of the Rokin, where the first-rate Reederij P. Kooij (who also have a jetty beside Centraal Station) offers all the basic cruises at competitive prices.

Information and maps

Information is easy to get hold of, either from the Netherlands Board of Tourism, via the Internet, or, after arrival, from any of the city's tourist offices, the **VVVs** (pronounced "fay-fay-fay"). There's a VVV tourist office on platform 2 at Centraal Station (Mon–Sat 8am–8pm, Sun 9am–5pm); a second, main one directly across from the main station entrance on Stationsplein (daily 9am–5pm); and a third on Leidsestraat, just off the Leidseplein (daily 9am–5pm). These three offices share one premium-rate information line on ⓣ0900/400 4040, and a website at ⓦwww.visitamsterdam.nl. They offer advice and information and sell a range of maps and guide books as well as tickets and passes for public transport. They also take in-person bookings for canal cruises and other organized excursions, sell theatre and concert tickets, and operate an extremely efficient accommodation reservation service for just €3 plus a refundable deposit which is subtracted from your final bill.

Maps

Our **maps** are more than adequate for most purposes, but if you need one on a larger scale, or with a street index, then pick up *The Rough Guide Map to Amsterdam*, which has the added advantage of being waterproof. This marks all the key sights as well as many restaurants, bars and hotels, but it does not extend to the outer suburbs. For this, the best bet is the Falk map of *Amsterdam* (1:15,000).

What's on information

For information about what's on, there's either the VVV (see above) or the **Amsterdam Uitburo**, the cultural office of the city council, housed in a corner of the Stadsschouwburg theatre on Leidseplein (daily 10am–6pm, Thurs until 9pm; ⓣ0900/0191). You can get advice here on anything remotely cultural, as well as tickets and copies of listings magazines. Amongst the latter, there's a choice between the AUB's own monthly *Uitkrant*,

Tourist passes

The VVV's much touted **Amsterdam Pass** provides free and unlimited use of the city's public transport network, a complimentary canal cruise and free admission to the bulk of the city's museums and attractions. It costs €26 for one day, €36 for two consecutive days and €46 for three, again consecutive, days. Altogether it's not a bad deal, but you have to work fairly hard to make it worthwhile. A much more tempting proposition, especially if you're staying for more than a couple of days, is the **Museumkaart** (museum card). This gives free entry to most museums in the whole of the Netherlands for a year; it costs €30, slightly less for both the under-25s and the over-60s.

which is comprehensive and free but in Dutch, or the VVV's bland *Day by Day in Amsterdam*. Alternatively, the newspaper *Het Parool*'s Wednesday entertainment supplement, *Uit en Thuis*, is one of the most up-to-date reference sources.

Banks and exchange

The easiest way to get money is to simply bring your **ATM** card and use it. However, for changing **travellers' cheques**, bank opening hours are Monday to Friday 9am to 4pm, with a few also open Thursday until 9pm or on Saturday morning; all are closed on public holidays. Outside these times, you'll need to go to one of the many **bureaux de change** scattered around town. GWK, whose main 24-hour branches are at Centraal Station and Schiphol airport, offers competitive rates and is very efficient. One cautionary word about other bureaux: some offer great rates but then slap on an extortionate commission, or, conversely, charge no commission but give bad rates. The VVV tourist office also changes money.

Lost and stolen credit cards and travellers' cheques

American Express Cards and cheques ⓣ020/504 8666
Mastercard ⓣ030/283 5555
Visa Cards and cheques ⓣ0800/022 4176

Communications

Post offices are open Monday to Friday 9am to 5pm, with the larger ones also open on Saturday mornings from 9am to noon. The main post office (Mon–Fri 9am–6pm, Thurs till 8pm, Sat 10am–1.30pm; ⓣ020/556 3311) is at Singel 250, on the corner with Raadhuisstraat. Current postal **charges** for a postcard or airmail letter (up to 20g) within the Netherlands is €0.39, €0.61 within the EU and €0.77 to the rest of the world. Stamps are sold at a wide range of outlets including many shops and hotels. Post boxes are everywhere, but be sure to use the correct slot – the one labelled *overige* is for post going outside the immediate locality.

Phones

Phone cards can be bought at many outlets, including post offices, tobacconists

Useful phone numbers

Operator (domestic and international) ☎0800 0410.
Directory enquiries: domestic ☎0900 8008; international ☎0900 8418.

and VVV offices, and in several specified denominations, beginning at €5. It is worth bearing in mind, however, that phone boxes are provided by different companies and their respective phone cards are not mutually compatible. KPN phones (and cards) are the most common. The cheap-rate period for international calls is between 8pm and 8am during the week and all day at weekends. Numbers prefixed ☎0800 are free, while those prefixed ☎0900 are premium-rated; a (Dutch) message before you're connected tells you how much you will be paying for the call. Finally, remember that although most hotel rooms have phones, there is almost always an exorbitant surcharge for their use.

Email and the Internet

Amsterdam is well geared up for email access with a healthy supply of Internet cafés. In addition, most of the better hotels provide email and Internet access for their guests at free or minimal charge.

Internet cafés

Conscious Dreams Kokopelli Warmoestraat 12 ☎020/421 7000, Ⓦwww.consciousdreams.nl. A smart shop offering Internet access and even DJs at the weekend. Daily 11am–10pm.
EasyInternetcafé Ⓦwww.easyeverything.com. This international chain has three Internet outlets in Amsterdam – one near Centraal Station at Damrak 33 (daily 9am–10pm); another at Reguliersbreestraat 22, near Rembrandtplein (same hours); and a third at Leidsestraat 24 at Keizersgracht (Mon 11am–7pm, Tues–Sat 9.30am–7pm & Sun 11am–6pm).
Het Internetcafe Martelaarsgracht 11 ☎020/627 1052, Ⓦwww.internetcafe.nl. Straightforward Internet café just 200m from Centraal Station. Reasonable rates – start up from just €0.50 – and open daily from 7am till late.

Opening hours

The Amsterdam weekend fades painlessly into the working week with many smaller shops and businesses, even in the centre, staying closed on Monday mornings until noon. Normal **opening hours** are, however, Monday to Friday 8.30/9am to 5.30/6pm and Saturday 8.30/9am to 4/5pm, and many places open late on Thursday or Friday evenings. Most restaurants are open for dinner from about 6 or 7pm, and though many close as early as 9.30pm, a few stay open past 11pm. Bars, cafés and coffeeshops are either open all day from around 10am or don't open until about 5pm; all close at 1am during the week and 2am at weekends. Nightclubs generally function from 11pm to 4am during the week, though a few open every night, and some stay open until 5am on the weekend.

Public holidays

Public holidays (*Nationale feestdagen*) provide the perfect excuse to take to the streets. The most celebrated of them all is Queen's Day – Koninginnedag – on April 30, which is celebrated with particular vim and gusto here in Amsterdam (see below).

January 1 New Year's Day
Good Friday (although many shops open)
Easter Sunday
Easter Monday
April 30 Queen's Day
May 5 Liberation Day
Ascension Day
Whit Sunday and Monday
December 25 and 26 Christmas

Festivals and events

Most of Amsterdam's festivals are music and arts events, supplemented by a sprinkling of religious celebrations and, as you might expect, the majority take place in the summer. The **Queen's Birthday** celebration at the end of April is the city's most touted and exciting annual event, with a large portion of the city given over to an impromptu flea market and lots of street-partying. On a more cultural level, the art extravaganza, the **Holland Festival**, held throughout June, attracts a handful of big names. Check with the VVV (see p.168) for further details.

January

Elfstedentocht (Eleven Cities' Journey) Annual ice-skating marathon across eleven towns and frozen rivers, in Friesland, starting and finishing in Leeuwarden. Held, weather permitting, sometime in January. Though the race had to be suspended for twenty years, a recent spate of cold winters has meant a number of competitions and an increasing number of participants – 16,000 is now the maximum number. For more details, call the organizers, De Friese Elfsteden, in the town of Leeuwarden (☎058/215 5020 11am–2pm, Ⓦwww.elfstedentocht.nl).

February

Chinese New Year **First or second week.** Dragon dance and fireworks, held at Nieuwmarkt.

Commemoration of the February Strike **February 25.** Speeches and wreath-laying at the Docker Statue on J.D. Meijerplein (see p.120).

March

Stille Omgang (Silent Procession) **Sunday closest to March 15 ☎023/524 6229.** Procession by local Catholics commemorating the Miracle of Amsterdam, starting and finishing at Spui and passing through the Red-Light District.

"Head of the River" rowing competition **Last week ☎035/577 1308, Ⓦwww.amsterdamscheroeibond.nl.** Actually three races along the River Amstel starting at 10am from Oudekerk to the centre and back; the last race, at 4pm, finishes near the *Amstel Hotel*.

April

Vondelpark Open Air Theatre **April–Aug ☎020/523 7790, Ⓦwww.openluchttheater.nl.** Free theatre, dance and music performances throughout the summer.

Nationaal Museumweekend **Second week ☎020/670 1111, Ⓦwww.museumweekend.nl.** Free entrance to most of the museums in the Netherlands.

Koninginnedag (the Queen's Birthday) **April 30.** This is one of the most popular dates in the Dutch diary, a street event par excellence, which seems to grow annually and is almost worth planning a visit around, despite some claiming it has become too commercialized over recent years. Celebrations for Queen Beatrix take place throughout the whole of Holland, though festivities in Amsterdam tend to be somewhat wilder and larger in scale. Special club nights and parties are held both the night before and the night after; however, to gain entry you'll need to book in advance either from the club itself or from selected record stores, such as Boudisque and Get Records. The next day sees the city's streets and canals lined with people, most of whom are dressed in ridiculous costumes (not surprisingly, Queen's Day is one of the most flamboyant events on the gay calendar as well). Anything goes, especially if it's orange – the Dutch national colour. A fair is held on the Dam, and music blasts continuously from huge sound systems set up across most of the major squares. This is also the one day of the year when anything can be legally bought and sold to anyone by anyone on the streets.

World Press Photo Exhibition Annual competition **Ⓦwww.worldpressphoto.nl.** Open to photographers from all over the world. Judging and award days take place mid-April, marking the beginning of the exhibition, which is held at the Oude Kerk until the end of May.

May

Herdenkingsdag (Remembrance Day) May 4. There's a wreath-laying ceremony and two-minute silence at the National Monument in Dam square, commemorating the Dutch dead of World War II, as well as a smaller event at the Homomonument in Westermarkt in honour of the country's gay soldiers who died.

Bevrijdingsdag (Liberation Day) May 5. The country celebrates the 1945 liberation from Nazi occupation with bands, speeches and impromptu markets around the city.

Oosterparkfestival First week. Held in the large park near the Tropenmuseum, this free festival celebrates the mix of cultures living in the area, with live music and numerous food stands.

World Wide Video Festival Mid-May to end May ⓣ020/420 7729, Ⓦwww.wwvf.nl. Celebrating small-screen culture with seminars on media art, screenings, exhibitions and meet-the-artist programmes. Held at the Passenger Terminal Amsterdam (PTA) situated on the River IJ, with smaller presentations at the Melkweg and the Dutch Institute for Media Art.

National Windmill Day Second Saturday ⓣ020/623 8703. Over half the country's remaining windmills and watermills are opened to the public. Contact Vereniging De Hollandsche.

Drum Rhythm Festival Second or third week Ⓦwww.drumrhythm.com. Amsterdam's first real summer event previously held over a weekend at the Westergasfabriek and very popular with locals. Famous musicians from all over the world take part, from Moby to Salif Keita. Sponsorship problems mean that they have yet to reschedule more dates, but check the website for the latest information.

KunstRAI Third week ⓣ020/549 1212, Ⓦwww.kunstrai.nl. The annual mainstream contemporary arts fair, held in the RAI conference centre, south of the centre. A less commercial alternative is the Kunstvlaai at the Westergasfabriek, always held the week before or after KunstRAI.

June

Holland Festival Throughout June ⓣ020/530 7111, Ⓦwww.hollandfestival.nl. The largest music, dance and drama event in the Netherlands, aimed at making the dramatic arts more accessible. Showcasing around thirty productions, it features a mix of established and new talent.

July

Beachbop Throughout July and August Ⓦwww.beachbop.nl. Live percussion, dance acts and plenty of beach parties at the Bloemendaal beach (close to Zandvoort). Friendly, low-key atmosphere; weekends only.

Over het IJ Festival First one or two weeks ⓣ020/771 3000, Ⓦwww.overhetij.nl. Modern theatre and dance festival held at the NDSM (ⓣ020/330 5480) in Amsterdam-Noord, across the river from the city centre. A festival boat runs there from behind Centraal Station.

Kwakoe Festival Weekends only from second week of July to second week of August Ⓦwww.kwakoe.nl. A Surinamese and Antillian festival held at a playground close to the Amsterdam ArenA in the southeastern suburbs, featuring lots of music, dance acts and stand-up comedy. There are also workshops, and even prayer services on Sunday morning. In the middle of the festival there's a football competition between several "tropical" teams. Caribbean delicacies such as *roti* and the Surinamese *bakabana*, baked banana with peanut sauce, are widely available from stalls around the festival.

August

Amsterdam Pride First or second weekend Ⓦwww.amsterdampride.nl. The city's gay community celebrates, with street parties and performances held along the Amstel, Warmoesstraat and Reguliersdwarsstraat, as well as a "Canal Pride" flotilla of boats cruising along the Prinsengracht.

Dance Valley First week ⓦwww.dancevalley.nl. Huge international dance event held over a weekend at the natural amphitheatre in the hills of Spaarnwoude, just north of Haarlem, with all the techno, drum-and-bass, house and ambient DJs you could possibly wish for. Check the website for further music events held here throughout the year.

The Parade First two weeks ⓣ033/465 4577, ⓦwww.mobilearts.nl. An excellent travelling theatrical fair with various short theatre performances given in or in front of the artists' tents (they all work independently). Held in the Martin Luther King Park, next to the River Amstel (from CS tram #25 to Hunzestraat), with a special kids' parade in the afternoons.

Uitmarkt Last week ⓦwww.uitmarkt.nl. A weekend where every cultural organization in the city advertises itself with free preview performances either on Museumplein or by the Amstel.

Grachtenfestival Last week ⓦwww.grachtenfestival.nl. International musicians perform classical music at twenty historical locations around the three main canals. Includes the Prinsengracht Concert, one of the world's most prestigious free open-air concerts, held opposite the *Pulitzer Hotel*.

September

Bloemencorso (Flower Parade) First week ⓦwww.bloemencorsoaalsmeer.nl. The Aalsmeer–Amsterdam flower pageant in the city centre, celebrating every kind of flower except tulips, which are out of season. Each year has a different theme. Vijzelstraat is the best place to see things, since the events in Dam square are normally packed solid.

Chinatown Festival Second weekend. Tong and Soeng musicians, acrobatics, kung-fu and tai-chi demonstrations at the Nieuwmarkt.

The Jordaan Festival Second or third week ⓣ020/626 5587, ⓦwww.jordaanfestival.nl. A street festival in the Jordaan, a friendly and fairly central neighbourhood. There's a commercial fair on Palmgracht, talent contests on Elandsgracht, a few street parties and a culinary fair on the Sunday afternoon at the Noordermarkt.

October

Amsterdam City Marathon Late October, usually the third weekend ⓦwww.amsterdammarathon.nl. A 42-kilometre course around Amsterdam starting at and finishing inside the Olympic Stadium, passing through the old city centre along the way.

November

Crossing Border Usually first week ⓣ020/346 2355, ⓦwww.crossingborder.nl. Festival centred around the Leidseplein area that explores and crosses artistic boundaries, with performances by over a hundred international acts presenting the spoken word in various forms, from rap to poetry.

Parade of Sint Nicolaas Second or third week. The traditional parade of *Sinterklaas* (Santa Claus) through the city on his white horse, starting from behind Centraal Station where he arrives by steam boat, before parading down the Damrak towards Rembrandtplein accompanied by his helpers the *Zwarte Pieten* ("Black Peters") – so called because of their blackened faces – who hand out sweets and little presents. It all finishes in Leidseplein on the balcony of the Stadsschouwburg.

Cannabis Cup Late November ⓦwww.hightimes.com. Five-day harvest festival organized by *High Times* magazine at the Melkweg (ⓣ020/531 8181), with speeches, music and a competition to find the best cultivated seed. Judging is open to the general public, but the entrance fee is pricey.

December

Pakjesavond (Present Evening) Dec 5. Though it tends to be a private affair, Pakjesavond, rather than Christmas Day, is when Dutch kids receive their Christmas presents. If you're here on that day and have Dutch friends, it's worth knowing that it's traditional to give a present together with an amusing poem you have written caricaturing the recipient.

The Winter Parade Last two weeks ⓣ033/465 4577, ⓦwww.mobilearts.nl. Winter version of the August Parade, except this one is held at the Westergasfabriek.

New Year's Eve Dec 31. New Year's Eve is big in Amsterdam, with fireworks and celebrations everywhere. Most bars and discos stay open until morning – make sure you get tickets in advance. This might just qualify as the wildest and most reckless street partying in Europe, but a word of warning: Amsterdammers seem to love the idea of throwing lit fireworks around and won't hesitate to chuck one at you.

Entertainment and nightlife

Although Amsterdam is not generally considered one of the world's major cultural centres, the quality and quantity of **music**, **dance** and **film** on offer are high – largely thanks to the government's long-term subsidy to the arts. For information about what's on, try the Amsterdam Uitburo, or AUB, the cultural office of the city council, which is housed in a corner of the Stadsschouwburg theatre on Leidseplein (daily 10am–6pm, Thurs until 9pm; ⓣ0900/0191). You can get advice here on anything remotely cultural, as well as tickets and copies of what listings magazines there are. A funkier outlet, however, is the Luckystrike shop in the Leidsestraat. Tickets for most performances can be bought at the Uitburo (for a €2 fee) and VVV offices, or reserved by phone through the AUB Uitlijn (ⓣ0900/0191 at €0.40p/m) for a one-percent booking fee, but the cheapest way to obtain tickets is to turn up at the venue itself.

Classical music and opera

There's no shortage of **classical music** concerts in Amsterdam, with two major orchestras based in the city, plus regular visits by other Dutch orchestras. The Royal Concertgebouw Orchestra remains one of the most dynamic in the world, and occupies one of the finest concert halls to boot. The other resident orchestra is the Netherlands Philharmonic, based at the Beurs van Berlage concert hall, which has a wide symphonic repertoire and also performs with the Netherlands Opera at the Muziektheater.

The most prestigious venue for opera is the Muziektheater (otherwise known as the Stopera) on Waterlooplein, which is home to the Netherlands Opera company – going from strength to strength under the guidance of Pierre Audi – as well as the National Ballet. Visiting companies sometimes perform here, but more often at the Stadsschouwburg and the Carré Theatre.

The most diverting multi-venue Dutch festival is the annual **Holland Festival** every June (see p.172). Otherwise, one of the more interesting music-oriented events is the piano recital held towards the end of August on a floating stage outside the *Pulitzer Hotel* on the Prinsengracht – with the whole area floodlit and filled with small boats, and every available spot on the banks and bridges taken up, this can be a wonderfully atmospheric evening.

Live music venues

Major **rock**, **folk** and **world music** venues include *Melkweg* (see p.102) and *Paradiso* (see p.102), while for **jazz** and **Latin music** head for *Akhnaton* (see p.86) or *Bimhuis* (see p.86).

Beurs van Berlage

Damrak 213 ⓣ020/627 0466, ⓦ**www.beursvanberlage.nl**. The splendid interior of the former stock exchange (see also p.70) has been put to use as a venue for theatre and music. The resident Netherlands Philharmonic and Netherlands Chamber Orchestra perform in the huge but comfortable Yakult Zaal and the AGA Zaal, the latter a very strange, glassed-in room-within-a-room.

Carré Theatre Amstel

115–125 ⓣ020/622 5225, ⓦwww.theatercarre.nl. A splendid hundred-year-old structure (originally built for a circus) which represents the ultimate venue for Dutch folk artists, and hosts all kinds of top international acts, notably touring orchestras and opera companies.

Concertgebouw

Concertgebouwplein 2–6 ⓣ020/671 8345, ⓦwww.concertgebouw.nl. After a recent facelift, the Concertgebouw is now looking – and sounding – better than ever. There are two halls here and both boast a star-studded international programme. Prices are very reasonable, rarely over €35, and €20 for Sunday-morning events. For more, see p.131.

Ijsbreker

Weesperzijde 23 ⓣ020/668 1805. ⓦwww.ijsbreker.nl. Out of the town centre by the Amstel, with a delightful terrace on the water. Has a large, varied programme of international modern, chamber and experimental music, as well as featuring obscure, avant-garde local performers.

Muziektheater

Waterlooplein ⓣ020/625 5455, ⓦwww.muziektheater.nl. Part of the €150 million complex that includes the city hall. The theatre's resident company, Netherlands Opera, offers the fullest, and most reasonably priced, programme of opera in Amsterdam. Tickets go very quickly. See also p.118.

Theatre

Surprisingly for a city that functions so much in English, there is next to no English-language **theatre** to be seen in Amsterdam. A handful of part-time companies put on two or three English productions during the summer and there are also occasional performances by touring groups, but pickings are thin. Try *Boom Chicago* (see p.101) for great improv **comedy**.

De Balie

Kleine Gartmanplantsoen 10 ⓣ020/623 2904, ⓦwww.balie.nl. A multimedia centre for culture and the arts, located off the Leidseplein, which often plays host to drama, debates, international symposia and the like, sometimes in conjunction with the *Paradiso* (see p.102) next door.

Dance

Amongst the several dance companies based in Amsterdam, the largest and most prestigious is the Muziektheater's National Ballet, under Wayne Eagling. Of the other major Dutch dance companies which frequently visit the city, the most innovative is The Hague's Netherlands Dance Theatre, with a repertoire of ballet and modern dance featuring the inspired choreography of Jiri Kylian and Hans van Manen.

On a smaller scale, Amsterdam is particularly receptive to the latest trends in modern dance, and has many experimental dance groups, often incorporating other media into their productions. Dance festivals are a little thin on the ground, with Julidans, held in the Stadsschouwburg every July, being the lead event.

Cosmic Theater

Nes 75 ⓣ020/622 8858, ⓦwww.cosmictheater.nl. A modern dance and theatre company featuring young professionals with a multicultural background.

Melkweg Theaterzaal

Lijnbaansgracht 234a ⓣ020/531 8181, ⓦwww.melkweg.nl. Upstairs in this pop and world music venue there's a little theatre with modern and funky productions.

Het Muziektheater

Waterlooplein ⓣ020/625 5455, ⓦwww.muziektheater.nl. Home of the National Ballet, but with a third of its dance schedule given over to international productions.

Film

Most of Amsterdam's commercial **cinemas** are huge, multiplex picture palaces showing a selection of general releases. There's also a scattering of film houses (filmhuizen) showing revival and art films and occasional retrospectives. All foreign movies playing in Amsterdam (almost no Dutch movies turn up anyway) are shown in their original language and subtitled in Dutch.

As a guide, tickets can cost around €7 for an evening show Friday to Sunday, though it's not hard to find a ticket for €5 during the week. Amsterdam's only regular film event is the fascinating International Documentary Film Festival in November/December (info ⊕020/620 1826, ⊛www.idfa.nl), during which 200 documentaries from all over the world are shown in ten days.

Cinecenter

Lijnbaansgracht 236 ⊕020/623 6615, ⊛www.cinecenter.nl. Opposite the *Melkweg*, this shows independent and quality commercial films, the majority originating from non-English-speaking countries. Shown with an interval.

Filmmuseum

Vondelpark 3 ⊕020/589 1400, ⊛www.filmmuseum.nl. The Filmmuseum holds literally tens of thousands of prints. Dutch films show regularly, along with all kinds of movies from all corners of the world. Silent movies often have live piano accompaniment, and on summer weekend evenings there are free open-air screenings on the terrace.

Kriterion

Roeterstraat 170 ⊕020/623 1708, ⊛www.kriterion.nl. Stylish duplex cinema close to Weesperplein metro. Shows art-house and quality commercial films, with late-night cult favourites. Friendly bar attached. Tram #6, #7, #10.

Melkweg

Lijnbaansgracht 234a ⊕020/531 8181 after 1pm, ⊛www.melkweg.nl. As well as music, art and dance (see p.102), the *Melkweg* manages to maintain a consistently good monthly film and video programme, ranging from mainstream fodder through to obscure imports.

The Movies

Haarlemmerdijk 161 ⊕020/624 5790, ⊛www.themovies.nl. A beautiful Art Deco cinema, and a charming setting for independent films. Worth visiting for the bar and restaurant alone. Late shows at the weekend.

Clubs

Clubbing in Amsterdam is not the exclusive, style-conscious business it is in many other cities. There is no one really extravagant night spot and most Amsterdam clubs – even the hip ones – aren't very expensive or difficult to get into. As for the music itself, Amsterdam is not at the cutting edge, with house still definitely the thing.

Although all the places listed in the guide **open** at either 10pm or 11pm, there's not much point turning up anywhere before midnight; unless stated otherwise, everywhere stays open until 5am on Friday and Saturday nights, 4am on other nights. For reviews of individual **venues**, see the end of each guide chapter.

For news and flyers about clubs, upcoming parties and raves, drop in to places like Clubwear House, at Herengracht 265 (⊕020/622 8766), and the Hair Police and Conscious Dreams, next door to each other at Kerkstraat 115 and 117.

Drugs

Thousands of visitors come to Amsterdam just to get stoned; in fact what most people don't realize is that all **soft drugs** – as well as hard – are technically illegal, it's just that possession and consumption have been partly decriminalized. Since 1976, the possession of small amounts of cannabis (up to 30g/1oz) has been ignored by the police, and sales have been tolerated to a selection of coffeeshops, where over-the-counter sales of cannabis are technically limited to 5g (under one-fifth of an ounce) per purchase. Outside of the coffeeshops, it's acceptable to smoke in some bars, but many are strongly against it so don't make any automatic assumptions. "Space cakes" (cakes baked with hashish and sold by the slice), although widely available, count as hard drugs and are illegal. And a word of warning: since all kinds of cannabis are so widely available in coffeeshops, there's no need to buy any on the street – if you do, you're asking for trouble. Needless to say, the one thing you shouldn't attempt to do is take cannabis out of the country – a surprising number of people think (or claim to think) that if it's bought in Amsterdam it can be taken back home legally. Customs officials and drug enforcement officers never believe this story.

Directory

Gay and lesbian Amsterdam Gay & Lesbian Switchboard ⓣ020/623 6565, ⓦwww.switchboard.nl (daily 2–10pm). For reviews of gay venues in the city, see the listings sections of each chapter.

Consulates UK, Koningslaan 44 ⓣ020/676 4343; USA, Museumplein 19 ⓣ020/575 5309.

Doctors/dentists Your hotel or the VVV should be able to provide the address of an English-speaking doctor or dentist if you need one.

Electricity 220v AC – effectively the same as British, although with round two- (or occasionally three-) pin plugs. British equipment will need either an adaptor or a new plug; American requires both a transformer and a new plug.

Emergencies Police, fire service and ambulance ⓣ112

Football Ajax Amsterdam ArenA stadium, ⓣ020/311 1444, ⓦwww.ajax.nl, metro Bijlmer; Feyenoord Rotterdam Olympiaweg 50, Rotterdam ⓣ010/292 3888, ⓦwww.feyenoord.nl.

Left luggage Centraal Station (daily 7am–11pm). Small coin-operated lockers cost €3.50, the larger ones €5.50 per 24 hours; left luggage costs €8 per item.

Mosquitoes These thrive in Holland's watery environment and are at their worst, as you would expect, near any stagnant or slow-moving stretch of water. Muggenmelk, with DEET, is very powerful: a little smear will keep them well away for a good night's sleep. Other popular brands include the Autan range. For more sensitive skins, Prrrikweg contains pungent citronella oil. After the event, an antihistamine cream such as Phenergan helps. All these and more are available all over Amsterdam.

Pharmacies You'll need an *apotheek* (usually Mon–Fri 9am–6pm, but may be closed Mon mornings) for minor ailments or to get a prescription filled. A complete list – with many opening hours – can be found in the city's yellow pages under "Apotheken". Most of the better hotels will be able to assist too.

Police Headquarters are at Elandsgracht 117 (ⓣ559 9111).

Tipping There's no necessity to tip, but a ten- to fifteen-percent tip is expected by taxi drivers and anticipated by many restaurant waiters.

Yellow pages The city's yellow pages are online at ⓦwww.goudengids.nl.

Language

Language

Dutch

It's unlikely that you'll need to speak anything other than English while you're in Amsterdam; the Dutch have a seemingly natural talent for languages, and your attempts at speaking theirs may be met with some bewilderment – though this can have as much to do with your pronunciation (Dutch is very difficult to get right) as their surprise that you're making an effort. Outside Amsterdam, people aren't quite as cosmopolitan, but even so the following Dutch words and phrases should be the most you'll need to get by. We've also included a basic food and drink glossary, though menus are nearly always multilingual, and where they aren't, ask and one will almost invariably appear.

Pronunciation

Dutch is pronounced much the same as English. However, there are a few Dutch sounds that don't exist in English, which can be difficult to pronounce without practice.

v like the English f in **f**ar
w like the v in **v**at
j like the initial sound of **y**ellow
ch and g are considerably harder than in English, enunciated much further back in the throat
ng is as in bri**ng**
nj as in o**nio**n
a is like the English **a**pple
aa like c**ar**t
e like l**e**t
ee like l**a**te
o as in p**o**p
oo in p**o**pe
u is like the French **tu** if preceded by a consonant; it's like w**oo**d if followed by a consonant
uu the French **tu**
au and ou like h**ow**
ei and ij as in f**i**ne
oe as in s**oo**n
eu is like the diphthong in the French **leur**
ui is the hardest Dutch diphthong of all, pronounced like h**ow** but much further forward in the mouth, with lips pursed (as if to say "oo")

Words and phrases

Basics and greetings

yes	ja
no	nee
Please	alstublieft
(no) thank you	(nee) dank u or bedankt
hello	hallo or dag
good morning	goedemorgen

good afternoon	goedemiddag
good evening	goedenavond
goodbye	tot ziens
see you later	tot straks
do you speak English?	spreekt u Engels?
I don't understand	Ik begrijp het niet
women/men	vrouwen/mannen
children	kinderen
push/pull	duwen/trekken

Getting around

how do I get to... ?	hoe kom ik in... ?
where is... ?	waar is... ?
how far is it to... ?	hoe ver is het naar... ?
when?	wanneer?
far/near	ver/dichtbij
left/right	links/rechts
straight ahead	rechtuit gaan
here/there	hier/daar

Ordering, shopping and money

I want...	Ik wil...
I don't want...	Ik wil niet... (+verb) Ik wil geen... (+noun)
how much is... ?	wat kost... ?
post office	postkantoor
stamp(s)	postzegel(s)
money exchange	geldwisselkantoor
cash desk	kassa
good/bad	goed/slecht
big/small	groot/klein
new/old	nieuw/oud
cheap/expensive	goedkoop/duur
hot/cold	heet or warm/koud
with/without	met/zonder

Days of the week

Monday	Maandag
Tuesday	Dinsdag
Wednesday	Woensdag
Thursday	Donderdag
Friday	Vrijdag
Saturday	Zaterdag
Sunday	Zondag

yesterday	gisteren
today	vandaag
tomorrow	morgen
tomorrow morning	morgenochtend
year	jaar
month	maand
week	week
day	dag

Numbers

0	nul
1	een
2	twee
3	drie
4	vier
5	vijf
6	zes
7	zeven
8	acht
9	negen
10	tien
11	elf
12	twaalf
13	dertien
14	veertien
15	vijftien
16	zestien
17	zeventien
18	achttien
19	negentien
20	twintig
21	een en twintig
22	twee en twintig
30	dertig
40	veertig
50	vijftig
60	zestig
70	zeventig
80	tachtig
90	negentig
100	honderd
101	honderd een
200	twee honderd
201	twee honderd een
500	vijf honderd
1000	duizend

Food and drink terms

Basics

boter	butter
boterham/broodje	sandwich/roll
brood	bread
dranken	drinks
eieren	eggs
gerst	barley
groenten	vegetables
honing	honey
hoofdgerechten	main courses
kaas	cheese
koud	cold
nagerechten	desserts
peper	pepper
pindakaas	peanut butter
sla/salade	salad
smeerkaas	cheese spread
stokbrood	French bread
suiker	sugar
vis	fish
vlees	meat
voorgerechten	starters/hors d'oeuvres
vruchten	fruit
warm	hot
zout	salt

Snacks

erwtensoep/snert	thick pea soup with bacon or sausage
huzarensalade	potato salad with pickles
Kkoffietafel	a light midday meal of cold meats, cheese, bread and perhaps soup
patates/frites	chips/French fries
soep	soup
uitsmijter	ham or cheese with eggs on bread

Meat and poultry

biefstuk (hollandse)	steak
biefstuk (duitse)	hamburger
eend	duck
fricandeau	roast pork
fricandel	frankfurter-like sausage
gehakt	minced meat
ham	ham
kalfsvlees	veal
kalkoen	turkey
karbonade	chop
kip	chicken
kroket	spiced veal or beef in hash, coated in breadcrumbs
lamsvlees	lamb
lever	liver
rookvlees	smoked beef
spek	bacon
worst	sausages

Fish

forel	trout
garnalen	prawns
haring	herring
haringsalade	herring salad
kabeljauw	cod
makreel	mackerel
mosselen	mussels
oesters	oysters
paling	eel
schelvis	haddock
schol	plaice
tong	sole
zalm	salmon

Vegetables

aardappelen	potatoes
bloemkool	cauliflower
bonen	beans
champignons	mushrooms
erwten	peas
hutspot	mashed potatoes and carrots
knoflook	garlic
komkommer	cucumber
prei	leek
rijst	rice
sla	salad, lettuce
stampot andijvie	mashed potato and endive
stampot boerenkool	mashed potato and cabbage
uien	onions
wortelen	carrots
zuurkool	sauerkraut

Cooking terms

belegd	filled or topped, as in *belegde broodjes* – bread rolls topped

	with cheese, etc
doorbakken	well-done
gebakken	fried/baked
gebraden	roasted
gegrild	grilled
gekookt	boiled
geraspt	grated
gerookt	smoked
gestoofd	stewed
half doorbakken	medium-done
hollandse saus	hollandaise (a milk and egg sauce)
rood	rare

Indonesian dishes and terms

ajam	chicken
bami	noodles with meat/chicken and vegetables
daging	beef
gado gado	vegetables in peanut sauce
goreng	fried
ikan	fish
katjang	peanut
kroepoek	prawn crackers
loempia	spring rolls
nasi	rice
nasi goreng	fried rice with meat/chicken and vegetables
nasi rames	rijsttafel on a single plate
pedis	hot and spicy
pisang	banana
rijsttafel	collection of different spicy dishes served with plain rice
sambal	hot, chilli-based sauce
satesaus	peanut sauce to accompany meat grilled on skewers
seroendeng	spicy shredded and fried coconut
tauge	bean sprouts

Sweets and desserts

appelgebak	apple tart or cake
drop	Dutch liquorice, available in *zoet* (sweet) or *zout* (salted) varieties – the latter an acquired taste
gebak	pastry
IJs	ice cream
koekjes	biscuits
oliebollen	doughnuts
pannekoeken	pancakes
pepernoten	Dutch ginger nuts
poffertjes	small pancakes, fritters
(slag)room	(whipped) cream
speculaas	spice and honey-flavoured biscuit
stroopwafels	waffles
taai-taai	Dutch honey cake
vla	custard

Fruits and nuts

aardbei	strawberry
amandel	almond
appel	apple
appelmoes	apple purée
citroen	lemon
druiven	grape
framboos	raspberry
hazelnoot	hazelnut
kers	cherry
kokosnoot	coconut
peer	pear
perzik	peach
pinda	peanut
pruim	plum/prune

Drinks

bessenjenever	blackcurrant gin
citroenjenever	lemon gin
droog	dry
frisdranken	soft drinks
jenever	Dutch gin
karnemelk	buttermilk
koffie	coffee
koffie verkeerd	coffee with warm milk
kopstoot	beer with a jenever chaser
melk	milk
met ijs	with ice
met slagroom	with whipped cream
pils	Dutch beer
proost!	cheers!
sinaasappelsap	orange juice
thee	tea
tomatensap	tomato juice
vruchtensap	fruit juice
wijn	wine
(wit/rood/rosé)	(white/red/rosé)
vieux	Dutch brandy
zoet	sweet

Index and small print

A Rough Guide to Rough Guides

Amsterdam DIRECTIONS is published by Rough Guides. The first *Rough Guide to Greece*, published in 1982, was a student scheme that became a publishing phenomenon. The immediate success of the book – with numerous reprints and a Thomas Cook prize shortlisting – spawned a series that rapidly covered dozens of destinations. Rough Guides had a ready market among low-budget backpackers, but soon also acquired a much broader and older readership that relished Rough Guides' wit and inquisitiveness as much as their enthusiastic, critical approach. Everyone wants value for money, but not at any price. Rough Guides soon began supplementing the "rougher" information about hostels and low-budget listings with the kind of detail on restaurants and quality hotels that independent-minded visitors on any budget might expect, whether on business in New York or trekking in Thailand. These days the guides offer recommendations from shoestring to luxury and they cover a large number of destinations around the globe, including almost every country in the Americas and Europe, more than half of Africa and most of Asia and Australasia. Rough Guides now publish:

- Travel guides to more than 200 worldwide destinations
- Dictionary phrasebooks to 22 major languages
- Maps printed on rip-proof and waterproof Polyart™ paper
- Music guides running the gamut from Opera to Elvis
- Reference books on topics as diverse as the Weather and Shakespeare
- World Music CDs in association with World Music Network

Visit **www.roughguides.com** to see our latest publications.

Publishing information

This 1st edition published August 2004 by **Rough Guides Ltd**, 80 Strand, London WC2R 0RL.
345 Hudson St, 4th Floor, New York, NY 10014, USA.

Distributed by the Penguin Group
Penguin Books Ltd, 80 Strand, London WC2R 0RL
Penguin Group (USA), 375 Hudson Street, NY 10014, USA
Penguin Group (Australia), 487 Maroondah Highway, PO Box 257, Ringwood, Victoria 3134, Australia
Penguin Group (Canada), 10 Alcorn Avenue, Toronto, Ontario, Canada M4V 1E4
Penguin Group (NZ), 182–190 Wairau Road, Auckland 10, New Zealand
Typeset in Bembo and Helvetica to an original design by Henry Iles.
Printed and bound in Italy by Graphicom

192pp includes index
A catalogue record for this book is available from the British Library

ISBN 1-84353-306-5

1 3 5 7 9 8 6 4 2

Help us update

We've gone to a lot of effort to ensure that the first edition of **Amsterdam DIRECTIONS** is accurate and up-to-date. However, things change – places get "discovered", opening hours are notoriously fickle, restaurants and rooms raise prices or lower standards. If you feel we've got it wrong or left something out, we'd like to know, and if you can remember the address, the price, the phone number, so much the better.

We'll credit all contributions, and send a copy of the next edition (or any other DIRECTIONS guide or Rough Guide if you prefer) for the best letters. Everyone who writes to us and isn't already a subscriber will receive a copy of our full-colour thrice-yearly newsletter. Please mark letters: "**Amsterdam DIRECTIONS Update**" and send to: Rough Guides, 80 Strand, London WC2R 0RL, or Rough Guides, 4th Floor, 345 Hudson St, New York, NY 10014. Or send an email to **mail@roughguides.com**

Have your questions answered and tell others about your trip at **www.roughguides.atinfopop.com**

Rough Guide credits

Text editor: Helena Smith
Layout: Dan May
Photography: Neil Setchfield
Cartography: Miles Irving
Picture editor: Jj Luck
Proofreader: Jan Wiltshire
Production: Julia Bovis
Design: Henry Iles
Cover art direction: Louise Boulton

The authors

Martin Dunford is one of the founders of the Rough Guide series and nowadays works as its Publishing Director, responsible for all Rough Guides travel publishing. In addition to Amsterdam, he has authored Rough Guides to The Netherlands, Belgium & Luxembourg, Brussels, Rome, Italy and New York.

Phil Lee has freelanced for Rough Guides for well over ten years. The other titles he has written for Rough Guides include Mallorca and Menorca, England, Norway, the Netherlands and Canada. He lives in Nottingham, where he was born and raised.

Acknowledgements

The authors would like to thank Karoline Densley for her tireless efforts to get everything right and Malijn Maat for her help and advice.

Photo credits

All images © Rough Guides except the following:

Front cover picture: © Robert Harding
Back cover picture: Keizersgracht © Alamy
p.2 Canal scene in Amsterdam © Dennis Degnan/Corbis
p.4 Tulips © Anthony Cassidy
p.4 Herengracht © Anthony Cassidy
p.7 Bike with flowers © Anthony Cassidy
p.8 Red Light District © Action Press (ACT)/Rex Features
p.12 Anne Frank House (© Anne Frank House);
p.18 Self portrait by Vincent van Gogh © Archivo Iconografico, S.A./Corbis
p.19 Patron at the Rijksmuseum © Adam Woolfitt/Corbis
p.19 Cobra Museum – Part of the exhibition room on the first floor, Cobra Museum for Modern Art Amstelveen. Photo: Kim Zwarts
p.22 Hans Brinker © Anthony Cassidy
p.22 Vondelpark © Anthony Cassidy
p.23 Flying Pig Palace © Anthony Cassidy
p.23 Bulldog © Anthony Cassidy
p.23 Meeting Point © Anthony Cassidy
p.23 International Budget Hotel © Anthony Cassidy
p.24 Keukenhof Gardens © Anthony Cassidy
p.24 Vondelpark © Anthony Cassidy
p.25 Hortus Botanicus © Dorling Kindersley
p.25 Zaanse Schans © Anthony Cassidy
p.26 Mazzo © Anthony Cassidy
p.27 Melkweg © Dorling Kindersley
p.27 Paradiso Club © The Cover Story/CORBIS
p.32 Parade of St. Nicolaas © Owen Franken/CORBIS
p.32 Gay parade © Richard Wareham/Sylvia Cordaiy
p.33 Cannabis Cup © Jeffrey L. Rotman/CORBIS
p.33 Queen's Birthday © Netherlands Tourism
p.34 Leliegracht © Anthony Cassidy
p.35 Brouwersgracht © Anthony Cassidy
p.35 Herengracht © Anthony Cassidy
p.35 Illuminated bridge © Netherlands Tourism
p. 40 Self Portrait as a Young Man, c.1628 (oil on panel) by Rembrandt Harmensz. Van Rijn (1606-69) © Rijksmuseum, Amsterdam Holland/Bridgeman Art Library
p.40 Self Portrait by Rembrandt Harmensz. Van Rijn (1606-69) © The Art Archive/Museo del Prado Madrid/Dagli Orti
p.41 The Night Watch, c.1642 (oil on canvas) by Rembrandt Harmensz. Van Rijn (1606-69) © Rijksmuseum, Amsterdam Holland/Bridgeman Art Library
p.41 The Jewish Bride, c.1666 (oil on canvas) by Rembrandt Harmensz. Van Rijn (1606-69) © Rijksmuseum, Amsterdam Holland/Bridgeman Art Library
p.50 Herring © Anthony Cassidy
p.50 Frites with sauce © Anthony Cassidy
p.51 Erwetensoep © Anthony Cassidy
p.51 Uitsmijter © Anthony Cassidy
p.51 Indonesian food – Nasi Goreng special © Anthony Cassidy
p. 54 Villa Zeezicht © Anthony Cassidy
p.54 Lunchcafé Winkel © Anthony Cassidy
p.54 Metz © Anthony Cassidy
p.64 Frozen canals, Keizersgracht © Anthony Cassidy
p.130 Woman Reading a Letter, c.1662-63 (oil on canvas) by Jan Vermeer (1632-75) © Rijksmuseum, Amsterdam, Holland/Bridgeman Art Library

Index

Map entries are marked in colour

S

t

V

W

Z

INDEX

low cost
hotels
with all the
frills...
...in amsterdam!
from £31*
up to
50% off
hotels' standard
rates
* per person per night based on 2 sharing a twin/double room with breakfast & taxes inc.
no booking fee!
up to 50% off hotels' standard rates
2 star to deluxe properties in 100 destinations
high-level service from friendly & knowledgeable staff
easy booking through our call centre or online
book now on:
0845 230 8888
www.hotelconnect.co.uk
ABTA ASSURED
hotelconnect
the hotel specialist